Soul Hunter

Soul Hunter

I'm only 16 years old just when I needed you the most
you all ran and left me alone in that house.

Sequoyah Hunter
Klingele

Printed in the United States of America
ISBN 978-1-958434-47-5 (sc)
ISBN 978-1-958434-48-2 (hc)
ISBN 978-1-958434-49-9 (e)

Library of Congress Control Number: 2022915936

2022.08.15

MainSpring Books
5901 W. Century Blvd
Suite 750
Los Angeles, CA, US, 90045

www.mainspringbooks.com

TABLE OF CONTENTS

INTRODUCTION

I am a soul hunter for God, of the unjust children living in the dark. My dad, who had to go into that evil drug shack where my mom lived. On a cold, dreary bone-chilling feeling of evil before midnight to identify his only son's murdered body. I was murdered by my mom, uncle, and his girlfriend with ten others. "I begged my mom to please take me from this evil house. I do not want to be around these people". And breaking my heart, she left me and watched me die from a drug overdose intentionally given to me. They were cleaning up the drug shack at 107 Recreation Dr. making excuses for each other and leaving my body for 16 hours. It broke my heart, and I did not want to go. I needed help; they ran and left me when I needed their help the most.

> Matthew 10; 34.— "Do not suppose that I have come
> to bring peace to the earth. I did not come to bring peace
> but a sword.

God needed an angel to show love, and there is the other side of God's love, God's wrath. Righteous indignation, and spiritual discernment, so run, run to hell. Soul Hunter, one by one, the Hunter will take them to hell for taking advantage of loving-kindness. God does not send anyone to hell. Psalms 104; 4.-Who makes his angels spirits; his ministers a flaming fire. The free will of our earthly desires will determine God's children's eternal destinations. We are judged on our thoughts, words, and what we do and fail to do.

> Matthew 7; 13 "Enter through the narrow gate. For wide
> is the gate and broad is the road that leads to destruction,
> and many enter through it. 14 But small is the gate and
> narrow the road that leads to life, and only a few find it.

Enter you in at the strait gate; for wide is the gate, and broad is the way, leading to destruction, and many go in thereat. Matthew 23; 33. "You snakes! You brood of vipers! How will you escape being condemned to hell?

There is a way to test the spirit of truth.

The unbelievers of the truth do not want examination. Suppose you criticize the unbelievers of truth if you endeavor to contend for the truth. If you expose their error, they will turn it around and condemn you as a sinner. If this is the actual work of the Holy Spirit, they would be inviting all the scrutiny they could get if they were honest and trustworthy.

They would want the affirmation and authentication if they were honest? Being deceitful and fraudulent in the error of their ways. You're the one standing in their way of the truth. In the Bible and the teaching of Jesus Christ our Lord, they have to turn in iniquity into a transgression against Christ for them to succeed. Sound doctrine proves that they do not survive.

Revelation 3; 3.—"Remember what you have received and heard; obey it, and repent. But if you do not wake up, I will come like a thief. You will not know at what time I will come to you."

Hebrews; 1; 13. To which of the angels did God ever say, "Sit at my right hand until I make your enemies a footstool for your feet"?

Ten thousand angels came with a bright light and drew me into heaven. I never knew what it was like to be free with this love of God. Such a miraculous dimension, the majestic beauty of heaven. God's love far exceeded my imagination or understanding. Very difficult to even explain the feeling. The measurement of God's love is so vast; that I can be with anyone instantly or simultaneously.

I am the guardian angel of the family, hockey players, friends, and family members that are God's divine creation and children of God. For the unjust and children who walk in the dark, think they got away with murder, run like hell, wherefore that's where the soul hunter will take you.

My 50% Native American Heritage, This is the only painting
I ever painted used for the front cover of this book

DEDICATION

Sequoyah Hunter dedicates this book from heaven supernaturally to my dad.

A special thanks to those who attended my service, gave their condolences, and called on the telephone. All the cards, loving, kind emails, and messages sent could not be measured. Baseball, football, hockey players, coaches, and the souls I love had many great memories and fun.

Great friends donated time building my hockey memorial at the high school and those hockey teammates who attended the memorial ceremony.

A special dedication to the country-western singer, J Smith, and the two young lady newspaper reporters, my aunt Kathy contacted from the worldwide press.

The outpour of love for Sequoyah Hunter and their family brings our hearts to tears. Thank you for being a part of my soul's journey. When I needed all of you the most with love and friendship, you were there.

CHAPTER 1

Two Fathers Devastated

About 9 PM Tuesday, a friend of my mom's came running into grandpa's home frantic and said that Sequoyah was dead. She appeared to be overreacting and emotional. It was all part of the setup. And being in a state of shock, Grandpa asked her, where? And what happened? And how? And she said, "Sequoyah was at his mom's home and said that he overdosed."

Grandpa immediately called his older daughter, and she was frantic and said, you're kidding me. Please tell me to tell me this is not true. And then grandpa called my dad on the telephone, and he said he would be right there. My dad was already on his way and already contacted.

My grandpa did not know where my mom lived. So this lady got into the passenger side of grandpa's car, and they drove from grandpa's home to the crime scene. It was a cold, freezing night, bone-chilling, possibly just the feeling of evil.

Driving on the way to the scene, Grandpa asks her where Sequoyah's mom is? And she said, "my mom said that I was sleeping on the couch when she left this morning. And she also said that my mom left for a city 200 miles away early that morning, at approximately 2 AM.

My mom's friend had told my grandpa the truth about the crime scene and named ten others. She also noted that my uncle and girlfriend were there. She also said that the homeowner was there with her son. They were having a party. With drugs, no doubt.

When arriving at the crime scene, the homeowner's son hit his fist on the tree in the middle of the driveway. Reflecting, no doubt, it was a setup for grandpa.

This is not what you would envision as being a drug house, completely remodeled, very well lit up with lights all around the home. A brand-new driveway, fresh paint on the home, and flowers are very well landscaped.

This lady got out of the passenger seat and said, "she had to get her car which she left in Grandpa's driveway."

The homeowner, a blonde lady, arrived standing off to the side of grandpa's vehicle next to her son. She had this look on her face like what was going on, one of a stage Hollywood scene. Grandpa thought this was not right, the way all these others at that home earlier were acting, in a fraudulent, evil disguise.

You would have thought the homeowner would come to give her condolences and see if there's anything she could do. Not attending my service with any of the others, and from what grandpa heard, the homeowner is in Hawaii. She was hiding on a boat in a nearby harbor for a while.

Who participated in my murder, cleaned up all the drug paraphernalia, and according to the Sheriff's Department, cameras were around the home and had all been removed. And made excuses for one another as deceitful fraudulent errors of their ways.

My dad arrived shortly after grandpa. He was getting into the passenger seat of grandpa's automobile. The deputies would not let anyone go into the crime scene.

Grandpa parked in the middle of the driveway; three deputies were there. Also, grandpa's niece and nephew were there with the law enforcement agencies. And grandpa's niece kept coming to the automobile, informing grandpa and telling his son precisely what was going on. Law enforcement agencies contacted grandpa's niece and nephew because they were connected through family connections.

Grandpa said to two of those officers, "you know if I were 100% able, I would be down there blowing breath into Sequoyah's lungs, and there's nothing you two gentlemen could do to stop me".

And one prominent officer said, "is there anything I can do for you"? And Grandpa said, "yes, bring my grandson back," Then Grandpa said, "excuse me, you gentlemen are doing an outstanding job."

My grandpa had priority; you could hear a whisper throughout the crowd that is Sequoyah's grandpa. One officer came up to my grandpa's car and asked him if he had some identification. My grandpa instantly gave him his driver's license.

My grandpa told my dad that this friend of my mom's said that I was asleep on the couch when my mom left that morning. My dad looked shocked after my dad said to grandpa, "that Sequoyah's mother said on the phone that she was in this city 200 miles away for two days".

How could she be gone in this city for two days? When she left her room when I was dead on the couch that morning? How can you be in two places at one time?

While grandpa was sitting in his automobile and his son in the passenger seat, Grandpa's nephew and a good family friend were just outside Grandpa's door.

My grandpa's stepson work for my dad, who I call my uncle. And the uncle arrived at the crime scene with an extra-large cowboy hat that appeared brand-new, and a cowboy scarf that looked brand-new. Uncle was clean shaving, look like he just had taken a shower. And he did not look like my uncle, and it appeared like he had stuffed his clothes to make him look muscular and much more significant. Nobody recognized him at first's appearance, was that different.

He seemed highly emotional when he arrived at the crime scene. He appeared to look as though he was 4 inches taller and could have had high heel cowboy boots on or boosters in his shoes to make him look bigger than life.

He ran over to my grandpa's door, yelling as loud as possible. What happened where is Sequoyah, immediately ran around to the passenger side of the car where my dad was sitting and did not stay but about 15 seconds. As my uncle was leaving the crime scene and on his way out, he turned around and shrugged his shoulders towards my dad. Later, my dad mentioned that to my grandpa. Shrugged his shoulders?

This means there is nothing I can do about your problem, or it's not my problem. Are you kidding me? And disappeared into the night, never to be seen again. For a simple reason, the authorities wanted the uncle, and there were warrants for his arrest when he saw the officers. This was all a setup because it was pitch black night, and it was all rehearsed before running into the scene.

Kind of strange that uncle and his girlfriend never separate. I'm sure his uncle's girlfriend coached him and had a rehearsal before the primary performance. They never attended my service or gave their condolences to the family.

My uncle, Being the stepson of grandpa, you would have thought the least he could do was be honest with the family. Like he had just come from the makeup set from a Hollywood scene. The makeup artist's uncle's partner in crime, his girlfriend.

The actor's name, the uncle of Sequoyah, was at the crime scene and participated in the crime with approximately ten others. This Hollywood acting was the worst ever witnessed by the director and movie producer.

Uncle instantly got back on his horse and rode off into the sunset. Of whom brought his nephew Sequoyah to his demise. Is uncle the horse riding cowboy guilty? Is Sequoyah's mother guilty? Are all unjust and blameworthy?.

> Proverbs 26; 3. A whip for the horse, a bridle for the ass, and a rod for the fools' back. Jeremiah 51; 21. And with you I break in pieces the horses and his rider; and break you into pieces that chariot and his rider. 2 Peter 2; 22. Of them the proverbs are true: "A dog returns to its vomit," and, "A sow that is washed returns to her wallowing in the mud."

My dad informed grandpa that he had legal custody of me, and my mom did not go near him because of heroin use.

The corner finally arrived and had to wait another 45 minutes until my dad was asked to come into the home by an officer to identify his son Sequoyah's body.

And Grandpa cannot even imagine what his son went through. Grandpa's son came running back to Grandpa's car with deep sobs. When my dad returned, he aged at least 20 years, something no two fathers should have to go through.

Both grandpa and his son were sobbing and trying to comfort each other and get a grip on what just happened. After some time, my grandpa stated to my dad that I was at peace now. And my dad said, "no", dad, he had the look of terror on his face with fear."

Just sitting in the vehicle in a total state of shock, my grandpa said to my dad, let's get out of here. I'm not going to watch my grandson be carried out of that house in a bag.

Grandpa and my dad left in their separate vehicles; my grandpa Followed my dad to Grandpa's house. Grandpa went into the house, and my dad stayed in his truck for about a half-hour before going to grandpa's home.

My dad finally came into the home; both grandpa and my dad sat there for about a half-hour, speechless in shock. When they finally had to say goodbye, they hugged each other as they had never before. And each of them said, I love you and held each other tightly.

Grandpa and his son are still in a state of shock, and when the anger mode gets into his son's head, Grandpa is afraid of what he is going to do. Grandpa knows this at present, the death of my only son and my only grandson Sequoyah.

Did Sequoyah go into the room his mother was renting and take drugs that killed him all by himself? With absolutely no one around? And the only drugs found throughout the entire drug house were in Sequoyah's backpack.

CHAPTER 2

The Request

Sequoyah's mom lives close by, and when Sequoyah first started staying at grandpa's humble home. Sequoyah would tell his grandpa he was going to his mom's house. Grandpa talking with my grandma, who lives in Oregon, concluded on the telephone one evening to let Sequoyah tell his dad about going to his mom's drug house. For this reason, if grandpa told Sequoyah's dad without giving Sequoyah notice first, it would most certainly create turmoil and chaos within the family.

And Grandpa thought about it, and Grandpa had a feeling that his son would not have wanted Sequoyah to stay at his mom's house. Because of her heroin addiction, crack, and whatever else. Grandpa said to Sequoyah, "if you do not tell your father that you are going to your mother's house, I will have to tell your father." Sequoyah said, "with a serious tone of voice, "please don't do that, grandpa.

I promise I will not go up there anymore". So assuming Grandpa could take Sequoyah for his word. Although young and impressionable very easily persuaded.

Sequoyah always told his grandpa when he was leaving, where he was going, and when he would be back. Grandpa agreed and consistently did not go completely asleep until his grandson was in for the evening. Grandpa agreed with Sequoia's request without reservation.

Let me say this about grandpa and their love for their grandchildren. This love that Sequoyah and his grandpa had between them was a love that cannot be applied to any other two souls on God's green earth. It was miraculous, supernaturally spiritual, in love, and a bond no one would ever understand except God, Sequoia, and his grandpa. A love that grandpa and grandson can only know.

Grandpas suddenly find out that their love for their grandchildren is far different from their children growing up. This is what is difficult for the children to understand. And even grandpa had to think about this difference in the love between child and grandchild. The love for your children is more disciplinary because they are your children.

The grandchildren, at least grandpa, reflect on his love for his grandson, Sequoyah. Grandpa's thinking and spiritually feeling inside that the disciplinary love should come from the parents, not the grandparents. At least not to yelling, grounding, and taking things from them for disciplinary time and spankings; it's more of a conversation that shows the grandparents' love for the grandchildren. And the grandchildren learn to respect the grandparents for what they say and do.

The only thing grandpa threatened Sequoia with would not be staying with grandpa anymore unless Sequoyah did not do what grandpa expected. It's more or less an understanding spiritually between grandchildren and grandparents. Respect has to be first, and most importantly, respect without reservation.

Grandpa's son expected grandpa to discipline Sequoia, like remembering when he was young. The sad part is that Sequoyah's dad may never get the opportunity; only God knows. This is why the last days of Sequoyah's life were the best days for grandpas. And grandpa's son will be with his son one day with unshakable faith.

CHAPTER 3

The Premonitions

"My uncles girlfriend and my uncle." Approximately four months before my demise, grandpa and my uncle's girlfriend went to the Veterans Administration hospital together early in the morning for an appointment my grandpa had. My uncle's girlfriend rode along to get the wheelchair out of the back of the car for my grandpa and push him into his appointment. And grandpa stipulated sternly to my uncle's girlfriend when I get out of my appointment, make sure you are here. My grandpa finished with his appointment, and the girlfriend was not there. My grandpa waited about 30 minutes and could see her driving from afar.

My grandpa was not happy, and she said she got lost and had to buy some underwear for herself.

My grandpa was steaming; as soon as my uncle's girlfriend put the wheelchair in the back of the car. Slamming the hatchback's rear down, my grandpa took off and left her standing there. Her purse, telephone, and everything were in the front passenger seat. She thought my grandpa would turn around, come back and pick her up, and she did not know my grandpa. Grandpa drove home without her.

My grandpa had a BB gun that my uncle had stolen from grandpa. My grandpa had an outside cat; it used to catch mice and was a real good mouser. One day the cat did not show up at all. It was somewhere else on the property and never came around the home again. My grandpa asked my uncle if he knew where his BB gun was? And my uncle said I don't know with guilt written over his face. My grandpa accused my uncle of shooting the cat with the BB gun, my uncle denied it, and my grandpa could see that he was lying in his eyes.

My uncle and his girlfriend lived in a shack next to my grandpa's. They were both drug users and thieves and robbed my grandpa blind. They took advantage of my elderly grandpa with one arm and a wheelchair 24 seven.

The straw that broke the camel's back was when my grandpa came out and found a crack pipe on the kitchen counter. My grandpa threw them both out of their shack and off the property.

My uncle and his girlfriend are a real sick combination. My uncle and her both use drugs and are both thieves and hoarders. She got my uncle prescription drugs, and in return, my uncle protected her. My uncle's girlfriend came into my grandpa's bedroom a couple of times when my uncle worked with my dad. And she asked my grandpa if he would like some company? And was touching him and rubbing him along his legs. She said, "everybody needs company once in a while. "And my grandpa said absolutely not, do not bother me, and please leave.

My uncle's girlfriend was so paranoid on one occasion from sleep deprivation that she was hallucinating. And said somebody was walking around on her roof and hiding in the trees. She even said to my grandpa don't you see them? They are right there? From long experiences, my grandpa knew precisely that she was paranoid, and from taking drugs, she had not slept in quite a few days, which caused hallucinations.

My uncle was working for my dad at the time and had to find somewhere to live. My dad agreed to get a debris box because my uncle was a hoarder. My dad ordered a 40-yard debris box, filling it to the top. And my grandpa had his caretaker screw the door shut so nobody else could live there. This was about two weeks before my murder. Grandpa knows from being around my uncle's girlfriend that she is cunning, deceitful, fraudulent, and evil. These are precisely the kind of people that killed me and set it up.

"Easter Sunday." 4 April 2021, Sunday at 10:10 AM. My grandpa, who I stayed with during the deliberate tragedy.

Two days before I was called home, it was Easter Sunday and my grandpa's birthday. My dad, grandpa, and grandpa all attended church together—a very small Catholic Church in grandpa's small town. Approximately 40 people were in attendance.

Sequoyah pushes up and down on his grandpa while his grandpa is in a deep sleep, saying, "wake up, grandpa, wake up. It's time to go to church." Both grandpa and Sequoyah looked at one another, smiling. Grandpa asked what time it was, and Sequoyah said 10:20 AM grandpa rolled over and went back to sleep and said, "the church does not start until 10:45 AM".

And grandson said, "it begins at 10:30 AM, grandpa; I just looked it up on my iPhone". Grandpa reluctantly woke up, adhering to his grandson's request. Grandpas think to himself, and it figures my grandson would be the only one to ever wake me up from a dead sleep and the only one that ever has. My grandson was a pleasure to be around and be with.

Sequoyah's dad was coming to pick them up. Grandpa drove his car, and his son met them at the church. Sequoyah and his dad went to church together on Easter Sunday, 4 April, because grandpa's birthday. Grandpa's grandson removed grandpa's wheelchair from grandpa's car and pushed grandpa into the church, where grandpa's son was waiting at the doorway for them.

Dipping their fingers in holy water and doing the sign of the cross entering the Catholic Church. Grandpa usually sits in the back row because it is more convenient in his wheelchair and does not disturb anyone. As the Holy Spirit would have it, there may have been only one person sitting on the aisle pews, directing them spiritually to the front pew. The front left pew was empty.

On the way out of the church, grandpa's son said, "why don't you let Sequoyah Drive"? It was not that far from their home, and Sequoyah did not have the experience of backing up. Grandpa's son looked a little disappointed.

Sequoyah loved his dad, grandpa, friends who lived in the area, and schooling. And he loved to play with grandpa.

After church, grandpa had his caretaker give Sequoyah a ride to work. Approximately 7 miles of winding mountain road to the restaurant. Sequoyah usually gets a ride home from a coworker, back to grandpa's home. Sequoyah considers grandpa's home to be his home, referring to grandpa as "my home," and considers his home with his dad "my dad's home or my home ." Having two homes always brought a smile to both grandpa and grandson.

4 April 2021, Sunday at 7 PM. After work, Sequoyah brought grandpa dinner that night from the restaurant. Grandpa remembers it was scrambled eggs with toast; it was perfect. Sequoyah always brings grandpas something home to eat from the restaurant. Then the grandson went into his room, the bathroom, the kitchen, and back and forth like a 16-year-old. And finally went into his room.

4 April 2021, Sunday at 7:30 PM. Sequoyah asked his grandpa if he could go to a friend's house for a couple of hours. And grandpa said that would be fine. Grandson left and came back about 11:50 PM. Said, I'm home, grandpa; good night, I love you. Grandpa's reply I love you, grandson; sleep tight; do not let the bedbugs bite, and say your prayers.

"The day before my murder" 5 April 2021, Monday at 2:05 PM. Grandpa went into Sequoyah's room and woke his grandson to go to the post office with grandpa to get the mail. One thing about Sequoyah, he wakes right up and is instantly ready to go, so if you ever wake him up, he does not need any time to get prepared. And he is always happy and says, I love you, grandpa. These are words grandparents love to hear. They cannot be told enough, especially to a grandfather who has other grandchildren who live hundreds of miles away and rarely sees them. It is always a pleasure for the grandparents, and it is never too for them to see their grandchildren.

As they drove out of the driveway, grandpa told his grandson that his caretaker would be leaving. Sequoyah said, "grandpa, I can rent that trailer and take care of you." Grandpa did not say anything. Sequoyah was on cloud nine, thinking that he would be able to live independently and take care of grandpa.

After arriving at the post office, Sequoyah said to grandpa, I have a $50 bill, grandpa, please stop at the store, and I will pay you the $10 IOU. And grandpa thought that was a great thought and made him responsible. Stopping at the store, the small store did not have change for the $50 bill. A friend of Sequoyah's was at the store, and his grandson said, this is my friend, grandpa. Grandpa introduced himself to Sequoyah's friends and dropped them off at the lake, Sequoyah always carried a backpack, and while he was getting out of grandpa's car, Sequoyah said I love you, grandpa, four times, and grandpa replied, I love you four times.

Grandpa thought it was strange that Sequoyah would say, I love you, four times. It was as though Sequoyah was saying goodbye to grandpa spiritually for the last time. Of course, Sequoyah always told his grandpa that he loved him. And grandpa would reciprocate.

Grandpa and Sequoyah had a check-in time no matter what. Call or, most importantly, come home and tell your grandpa where you are. That was 8 PM on the nights Sequoia stayed with grandpa on the weekends.

5 April 2021, Monday at. At 8 PM, Sequoia came in, saying I'm home grandpa went into his room. Grandpa was busy on the computer. Grandpa is a published author (herbklingele.com) on the computer, mainly researching the Bible or theology, history, editing, writing, and journaling.

Grandpa did not reciprocate because he was busy on a project. Sequoia could see grandpa walking down the hallway towards grandpa's computer desk. Grandpa can see Sequoia in his peripheral vision and is aware of his presence. Sequoia stayed in his bedroom for a few minutes, came out, and mentioned that he was going to a friend's house for a couple of hours, and grandpa said, okay, grandpa never looked up at his grandson. And he said, I love you, grandpa, and Grandpa said, I love you too.

You never know when it is the last time you will hear someone's voice that you love very much. More than anyone in the whole wide world, and the last thing you expect is for them never to return.

CHAPTER 4

The Devil is a Murderer and Liar

And here's the question and the answer.

Question: "Is the devil/Satan a person or a force/personification of evil?"

Answer: Although he has persuaded many people that he doesn't exist, Satan is a real, personal being, the source of all unbelief and immoral and spiritual evil. He is called by various names in the Bible, including Satan (meaning "adversary"—

> Job 1; 6.—Now there was a day when the sons of God came to present themselves before the LORD, and Satan also came among them. Romans 16; 20.—And the God of peace shall bruise Satan under your feet shortly. The grace of our Lord Jesus Christ is with you. Amen.

The Devil "Slanderer."

> Matthew 4; 1.—Then Jesus led the spirit into the wilderness to tempt the devil. Isaiah 14; 12.—the serpent, 12, How art thou has fallen from heaven, O Lucifer, son of the morning! How art thou cut down to the ground, which didst weaken the nations! the serpent. 2 Corinthians 11; 3.—But I fear, lest by any means, as the serpent beguiled Eve through his subtilty, so your minds should be corrupted from the simplicity that is in Christ. Revelation 12; 9.— And the great dragon was cast out, that old serpent, called the devil, and Satan, which deceiveth the whole world: he was cast out into the earth, and his angels were cast out with him.

And many others.

The existence of Satan as a personal being is proved by the fact that the Lord Jesus Christ recognized him as such. Jesus referred to him frequently by name. Luke 10; 18. He said unto them that I beheld Satan as lightning falls from heaven.

> Matthew 4; 10.—Then saith Jesus unto him, Get thee hence, Satan: for it is written, Thou shalt worship the Lord thy God, and him only shalt thou serve. and called him "the prince of this world." John 12; 31.—Now is the judgment of this world: now shall the prince of this world be cast out. 14; 30.—Hereafter, I will not talk much with you: for the prince of this world cometh, and hath nothing in me.

16; 11.—Of judgment, because the prince of this world is judged. The apostle Paul called Satan the "god of this world."

2 Corinthians 4; 4.-In whom the God of this world hath blinded the minds of them which believe not, lest the light of the glorious gospel of Christ, who is the image of God, should shine unto them, infant memory clean three pleadings enacted and the "prince of the power of the air." Ephesians 2; 2.—Wherein in time past ye walked according to the course of this world, according to the prince of the power of the air, the spirit that now worketh in the children of disobedience:

> The apostle John said, "The whole world is under the control of the evil one."

1 John 5; 19. We know that we are of God and the whole world lieth in wickedness and that Satan "leads the whole world astray." These could hardly be descriptions of an impersonal force or a mere personification of evil.

The Scriptures teach that God had created an "innumerable company of angels before man and the world were created."

Hebrews 12; 22.—But ye have come unto mount Sion, and unto the city of the living God, the heavenly Jerusalem, and an innumerable company of angels, a heavenly host of spiritual beings of great strength and intelligence. The highest of these beings are the cherubim, who are attendants at the very throne of God, and the "anointed cherub" was initially Satan himself.

> Ezekiel 28; 14. Thou art the anointed cherub that covereth, and I have set thee so: thou wast upon God's holy mountain; thou hast walked up and down amid the stones of fire.

He was "full of wisdom and perfect in beauty."

CHAPTER 5

Lawlessness

"Sin is the transgression of the law. To sin is to transgress,
or break, the law of God. All have sinned (Romans 3:23),
and that sin leads to death (Romans 6:23). 1 John 3:4:

To sin is to miss the goal or target. It is to fall short of what God expects of us. Sin is the opposite of righteousness. Righteousness is living within God's just and reasonable standards, while sin fails to live by those standards. Is without or against the law. "Lawlessness" to live or conduct oneself as if there is no law.

Sin is making a decision—or living a lifestyle—that misses the mark and violates the law of God. It can also mean to "turn away" rebellion or revolt or sin. 2 Chronicles 24:20, "The Spirit of God came upon Zechariah the son of Jehoiada, the priest, who stood above the people, and said to them, 'Thus says God: "Why do you transgress the commandments of the LORD so that you cannot prosper?"

"Blessed is he whose transgression [rebellion, sin] is forgiven, whose sin is covered" (Psalm 32:1). So when our transgressions and sins are forgiven, our rebellion and revolt against God are removed from us. God's primary laws to guide human conduct are the 10 Commandments (Exodus 20).

We can transgress those laws in two ways: Live a general lifestyle of lawlessness. This means we live a self-willed way of life without any thought or care for the restraints of God's law. For instance, people who make all their decisions according to their passions or desires live in a lawless condition. We can transgress a specific commandment. God's law instructs us to "not steal" (Exodus 20:15). If we ignore that law and steal something, we have transgressed the law—and sinned.

Both the general lifestyle of sin and committing specific acts of sin bring undesirable consequences. "When we live within God's 10 Commandments, we free ourselves from suffering caused by breaking those commandments.

"God's law was given to show humankind the best way to live in harmony with God and others (Luke 10:27). God gave the law a blessing and intended it to guide humanity into an abundant way of life (John 10:10). He wants all people to have prosperity, peace, and joy in their lives.

Did Jesus uphold the law of God, or did He do away with the commandments? He answered that question directly in the Sermon on the Mount: "Do not think that I came to destroy the Law or the Prophets. I did not come to destroy but to fulfill" (Matthew 5:17).

"Fulfill" means the opposite of "destroy." He gave full meaning to the law and summarized it into two overall great commandments.

When a man asked Him, "Which is the great commandment in the law?" Jesus answered, "'You shall love the LORD your God with all your heart, with all your soul, and with all your mind.' This is the first and great commandment. And the second is like it: 'You shall love your neighbor as yourself'" (Matthew 22:36-39).

These two great commandments are God's 10 Commandments. The first four commandments state how we are to love God. The last six commandments say how we should treat one another. Breaking any of these commandments is a sin.

God established blessings for obedience to His law and penalties for disobedience (Deuteronomy 28:1-2, 15). God has designed human life to work best when aligned with His law. Obedience so that other peoples would learn to obey and be blessed.

Just as modern nations today do not obey God. The world exists in a state of sin and continues to write a sad, violent history.

A time is coming when Jesus Christ will return to rule the earth and end moral confusion. He will establish God's law as the law of the world. All people will come to understand the law. They will learn what sin is and what the consequences of lawlessness are. Of course, people will still be people—there will be sins that must be forgiven. But they will be led by a moral upright, and will experience righteousness, peace, and joy.

People everywhere will love the law and the rewards for obeying it. In the future government of Jesus Christ, the prophecy of Jeremiah will be fulfilled: 'Obey My voice, and I will be your God, and you shall be My people. And walk in all the ways I have commanded you, that it may be well with you" (Jeremiah 7:23).

"Whatever is not from faith is sin" (Romans 14:23). To him who knows to do good and does not do it, to him it is a sin" (James 4:17). "All unrighteousness is sin" (1 John 5:17). Unfaithfulness to God can also be neglecting to do what's right when we have the opportunity.

Sin is against God, and it brings the death penalty (Romans 6:23; But God provides a way we can have that penalty removed through the sacrifice of Jesus Christ: "Who Himself bore our sins in His own body on the tree, that we, having died to sins, might live for righteousness" (1 Peter 2:24).

When we accept Christ's sacrifice and have our sins washed away through baptism, we cease being slaves to sin and become slaves of righteousness (Romans 6:17-18). Righteousness is the opposite of lawlessness. It strives to live within the boundaries of God's law (Psalm 119:172).

We can experience a great measure of peace and stability in keeping God's law. "Moreover by them [the law, testimony, statutes, commandments and judgments] Your servant is warned, and in keeping them there is great reward" (Psalm 19:11). "But let your heart keep my commands; for length of days and long life and peace they will add to you" (Proverbs 3:1-2).

CHAPTER 6

Hell

Hell is separation from God eternally. Punishment of the Wicked. The Kingdom of God, Jesus Christ spoke a parable about wheat and tares growing together in the same field until the harvest, when they would be separated (Matthew 13:24-30). After sending the multitude away (verse 36), Jesus told His disciples that this harvest represented "the end of the age" (verse 39) when angels would reap the harvest of people for the Kingdom.

The "lake of fire". Jesus explained that in this harvest the angels would "gather out of His kingdom all things that offend, and those who practice lawlessness, and will cast them into the furnace of fire. There will be wailing and gnashing of teeth" (Matthew 13:41-42).

This "furnace of fire" is also referred to in Scripture as "the lake of fire" (Revelation 20:15), where those whose names were not written in the Book of Life will be cast. The punishment of the wicked—those who will not repent of their sins—is to be burned up.

Prophet Malachi, "'For behold, the day is coming, burning like an oven, and all the proud, yes, all who do wickedly will be stubble. And the day which is coming shall burn them up,' says the LORD of hosts, 'that will leave them neither root nor branch'" (Malachi 4:1). Continuing, God says to the righteous, "'You shall trample the wicked, for they shall be ashes under the soles of your feet on the day that I do this,' says the LORD of hosts" (verse 3).

Because of the mistaken idea that humans have an immortal soul, many have likewise mistakenly assumed that the wicked will suffer eternal torment in an ever-burning fire. But this is not what the Bible teaches. Instead, unrepentant humans will be mercifully destroyed.

Sequoia Hunter Klingele - 16 years old victim of drug-induced homicide. Found dead 6 April 2021 at 103 Recreation Dr., La Honda, CA. (A known drug house where 911 records indicate a week earlier a young female overdosed).

My mom stole this prescription bottle from a lady she knew who died of cancer and broke into her home when nobody was in the house. Half of this bottle was sold to me for $50 by my uncle and his girlfriend. The second half of this bottle was sold on Snapchat two days later with the tag saying, "who needs the rest?"

He was poisoned to death with stolen prescription methadone.

Being sold on Snapchat by username "Anthony Salvi," the Italian" "Anthony."

The distribution of a controlled substance that results in death is a federal crime. To sell or give a prescription drug to another person without a license is a federal crime. Maintaining drug-involved premises is a federal crime. Knowingly and willingly making a material false statement to law enforcement is a federal crime. **Up to $20,000 reward.** If your tip and testimony directly lead to the arrest and conviction of the person (s) for a felony crime related to my death. Citizens are urged to come forward with any facts or circumstances about this crime and information on legal activity at 103 Recreation Dr., La Honda, CA 94020. Call or text tip line 650-466-8055. Old drug dealers accountable. Help shut a drug house down. You may save the life of a child!

God did not create Satan as an evil being, however. The angels, like man, were created as free spirits, not as unthinking machines. They were entirely able to reject God's will and rebel against His authority if they chose.

The fundamental sin is the twin sin of unbelief and pride in man and angels. Satan said in his heart, "I will ascend into heaven, I will exalt my throne above the stars of God . . . I will be like the highest." Isaiah 14; 13.—For thou hast said in thine heart, I will ascend into heaven, I will exalt my throne above the stars of God: I will also sit upon the mount of the congregation, in the sides of the north:14, I will ascend above the heights of the clouds; I will be like the highest. Again, these could hardly be the actions or motivations of an impersonal force.

Jesus also told us of some of the characteristics of Satan. Christ said he was a murderer from the beginning, not holding to the truth, for there is no truth in him, and that when he speaks, he lies, he speaks his native language, for he is a liar and the father of lies.

Christians must recognize the reality of Satan and understand that he prowls around like a roaring lion looking for someone to devour. 1 Peter 5; 8.-Be sober, be vigilant; because your adversary the devil, as a roaring lion, walketh about, seeking whom he may devour:

It is impossible to overcome sin and temptation by the devil, but Scripture tells us how to be strong. We need to put on the whole armor of God and withstand the temptation. Ephesians 6; 13.—Wherefore take unto you the whole armor of God that ye may be able to withstand in the evil day and having done all, to stand.

Not one omen owed to God shall go unpaid. Nowhere in the Bible have I read to forgive Satan or pray for the Snake; if you're not growing along spiritual lines and stuck, continuously looking in your rearview mirror, you would not know that.

Proverbs 26; 11. As a dog returns to his vomit, a fool returns to his folly. Sometimes it's not what you know; it's who you know.

CHAPTER 7

Revealed

My dad was at a local store late one night, turned the corner, and pumped right into a friend of my mom's who showed my grandpa where my mom lived. Then later denied it. My dad called my grandpa from the store, and my dad wanted my grandpa to talk to this lady and get her to tell the truth. My grandpa did not recognize my dad's voice on the telephone.

And the first question my grandpa always asked was, "Why were you not at my grandson's service"? She instantly lied and said that she had never heard about the service or when and where it would be. My grandpa told her she was a liar, and she instantly handed the telephone back to my dad. After hanging up with my grandpa, my dad told her specifically, "if I ever see you again, I will kill you."

She only lives in the same small town everybody else lives in. My grandpa asked them that question to hear them lie.

On Facebook, some lady contacted my grandpa, a good friend of grandpa's stepdaughter, my uncle's sister. Right after I was murdered and "said I heard your grandson overdosed on drugs" early in the morning? And that's where my mother ran to hide.

God's love and God's wrath work both ways. It's the simple, "if you do good things, good things happen." "If you do bad things, bad things happen."

Grandpa's unshakable faith is praying one evening. As usual, the telephone rang, and it was a professional offered his services, said patiently when the dust settled one by one and hung up. So run, run like hell. Isn't it strange that not one of those evil souls in that home, or at that party, even offer their condolences to the family? Be patient, be free, have fun, and please enjoy the short life you have in front of you for the dogs that return to their vomit.

Although God had a love to show many others by taking Sequoyah by the hand.

James; 2;19. Thou believe that there is one God; thou doest well: the devils also believe and tremble.

John 8; 44.—Ye are of your father the devil, and the lusts of your father ye will do. He was a murderer from the beginning and abode not in the truth because there is no truth in him. He speaks of his own when he lies: he is a liar and its father.

What mother murders her son? What uncle participates in the murder of his nephew with his girlfriend. What homeowner and her son provide a home for murderers? What so-called friend participates in the murder with others? God help my mom, my uncle, and the uncle's girlfriend. A 16-year-old child in the presence of all adults over 18 years of age, especially my mom, who did not have custody of me. It sounds to Grandpa like his only grandson was murdered by the mom. The mother should have had the maturity to know that she was not supposed to be in the presence of her son. You would think they would not introduce me to a drug cocktail that killed me.

It is for all the people at the location, while one or all of them had given Grandpa's grandson Sequoyah the wrong combination of drugs. Isn't it strange how somebody ODs in a house, all the unjust and children of the dark scatter and hide? Sometimes it's not what you know; it's who you know.

All liars and thieves are guaranteed a trip to hell. Revelation 21; 8. But the fearful, unbelieving, and abominable, and murderers, and whoremongers, and sorcerers, and all liars, shall have their part in the lake which burns with fire and brimstone the second death.

Of course, my mom and my uncle's girlfriend, especially my uncle and acquaintances, killed me. They left me alone in that house just when I needed them the most they ran like rats. All I did was love everyone and found out that the ones I thought loved me ran like rats and rodents fraudulently and treacherously. Betrayal is the lowest level of hell.

If they confess and forsake their sins, never do them again, and the truth shall set them free. And only God knows their hearts and eternal destination.

CHAPTER 8

Anonymous

Anonymous

16 April 2021. I found out who it was that your grandson got the drugs from. It was a friend who died of pancreatic cancer. I went and sat on the beach this morning and mourned her passing. I am sad for her beautiful lovely good children, what special children she has had. But I am so isolated here I don't find out anything until much late. That's right. I never could get that name right, never not in all these decades and decades. How many people will get that one, right? Seriously?

I did not hear anything until last night. I attended all of her other family member's services and did not participate in hers. Nobody told me I felt so guilty, and yukky did not pay my respects, but how was I to know if nobody told me? I have been friends with her family since I was 12 years old. She s dead. I missed her service.

She didn't get them from her, and she stole them from her, don't forget that. She stole from a dying person. How despicable.—Things are all bad, but she should be punished if she harbors your grandson's mother. The friend with your grandson's mother, my husband, hates her guts, no, no no, you see your grandson's mother's daughter lives next door to your grandson's friend's mom, same trailer park, same section, same street.

The side practically sides the spaces. Your grandson's mother's friend is afraid of your grandson's mother, so she pretends to be friends with her. She hates her guts too. But I will find out—either way. I hate your grandson's mother so much and never hate anything or anyone, and there are my top 10 people I hate because they are murderers, rapists, pedophiles, & the like. I hate Satan & she is Satan's concubine, a Jezebel riding the seven-headed beast of Babylon.

She did things to my baby & me that are unforgivable. I swore I'd kill her. Oops, did I say that??? I guess it's the Siciliano. It's In My DNA I never forget a wrong against my child or my home, my kindness, hospitality, or generosity. She mistook my kindness for weakness—a big mistake. I've swung an ax at her head a few times. The only way to kill something without a soul is to decapitate it, drive a stake through its chest, bury the head far away from the body, or wait, am I thinking of the undead like? Vampires.

Oh, well, the same thing. I'd cut off some fingers and toes just for an opportunity to take that evil soulless, godless, soul-sucking c*** down & I only reserve that word for those who are very, very special.

I loathe her. Beyond that, She did something against my daughter when she was just a tiny baby. I will never forgive that.

My home nonetheless, She's been on my shit list, for, let us see. Umm . . . 22 & 1/2 years now. Her other son had not talked to her in, I guess, a while & he was in distress over his newborn baby & as soon as she got off the phone with him, he was dead within 8 minutes or less of that call & he was in Northern Canada, her EVIL reaches far far away.

She did so wrong that he forgot he even had a baby, just like her. She cranks them out for the tribal welfare money. So what's one more or one less to her? She truly is what I call evil. I save that word only for particular persons as well. Not a term I use loosely, mind you. If she is there, your grandson's monitors friend deserves what's coming to her, and her whole family can go into the klink.

Do you know the homeowner where your grandson's body was found? A blonde girl plays guitar, and your grandson's mother stays there all of the time. Those two are in real cahoots. Es she robbed her blind, who the hell steals a baby blind? Who in the hell does that kind of stuff? She did things to me that permanently affected my life.

It even affected my education in college when I went back to better myself and train for a real career. Wow, right . . ? I mean lasting repercussions that went on and on and on and ad infinitum, okay, I will find out if she is in Selma, but I think she's just a hop skip jump away from you personally.

She got no conscience, nothing, just a black sucking hole that robs rooms of oxygen. People like us need she is a waste of damn oxygen and space on this planet. She is so evil I bet the earth would vomit her right back out. She could never be buried because the world hates such dark, pure, unadulterated EVIL.

My typing sucks. I'm not wearing glasses. Okay, that's all I know, I will ask around, but that doesn't mean I will have any answers, give me about 24 hours or less. As soon as I find out anything, you will be the first to know. She kills two young men in less than one year, an incredible, true gorgon. All they have to do is hear her voice or see her face, and they drop dead within minutes of that encounter. Absolutely. Uncanny, incredible, in a wrong way. Wow. Right. Enough to GOD—SMACK a soul that thought, okay, Uncle.

I will get back to you regardless. Your grandson's mother's friend, that was with her at the time of the murder is the person who called me crying and told me the news. I was not a bit surprised. I did not even raise an eyebrow. It was so far from the source, no offense to your family.

Anything that evil harpy does not surprise me, no matter how outrageous and cruel and black-hearted.

Anonymous

Sent 8 August 2021.
Yes, I told her when your son is saying to you, "please don't leave". I have nightmares of it. I can still hear his (Sequoyah) voice.

Sent August 8 at 12:04 PM.

I know, and I will say that I have information that will have Jennifer arrested.

My mom did not know that a close friend with my mom at the house could not handle the guilt and witnessed everything.

I said, "DO NOT LEAVE ME HERE IN THIS HOUSE WITH THOSE PEOPLE; PLEASE, MOM, TAKE ME WITH YOU." IT BROKE MY HEART THAT MY MOM DID NOT HELP ME AND LEFT.

This collaborated with an eyewitness. This so-called friend of my mom's said to my mom, "YOU JUST CAN NOT LEAVE SEQUOYAH HERE IN THAT CONDITION. TAKE HIM DOWN TO HIS GRANDPA'S."

She also said when talking to grandpa on the telephone. That Sequoyah could not move because of the drug (methadone) was given. An excessive amount killed (murdered) Sequoyah.

Sequoyah asked his mother not to leave him there with ten others in the home, knowing that Sequoyah would die from the overdose he was given.

They all started cleaning up the house, taking down the cameras, and making excuses.

Writing this and thinking about this is sad what my grandson must have been going through. And Sequoyah's mother and friend left for Fresno, California. This is where the mother's friend resides. The only drugs found in the house were in Sequoyah's backpack.

The friend of my grandson's mother cannot handle the guilt in the first two sentences is what she had written on Facebook. Not only that, Sequoyah's grandfather called her on the telephone for a half-hour telephone conversation. She was admitting that everybody was walking around Sequoyah's body, cleaning up, making excuses, and leaving his body in that house, before a friend of Sequoyah's got suspicious and found the body of my grandson.

This lady on the telephone was shaking so badly and was in total disbelief of what Sequoyah's mother would do. Sequoyah's mother had told Sequoyah's father that she was 200 miles away at the incident (murder).

The local sheriff's department should be held accountable for their unprofessional lack of investigation.

Grandpa has one question for the authorities, why has grandpa not been investigated? The last place my grandson was living? The DEA the local County Sheriff's Department?

Anonymous

17 March 2022. On another subject, Sequoyah's mother killed her other son remotely. You know she admitted to me her murder of her last two or three husbands. She is a black widow, to be sure. She said, 'You see that red truck? I killed my last husband for it. I put a pillow over his face when he was sleeping. I'm like, wow, are you sure you want to be telling me this? She's said: who cares? Nobody can prove it Was me, ha ha ha ha, and she laughs maniacally; then she stole all my infant daughter's money FROM HER

PIGGY BANKS and investment jewelry, diamond, and gold I invested for her for when she's older. Who rips off an infant??!

A CERTIFIED MONSTER, THAT'S WHO!! SHES is living at Pope Road. Now you know, I can only give you past information. I cut MYSELF off recently from EVERYONE.

She's living with Scott, a known dealer of illicit drugs, mainly cocaine, and possibly involved in his partner in 2019. So they deserve one another.

She had sex with animals in exchange for narcotics. You know, no self-respect, she a black hole of greed need and SF loathing you know she has no life force emanating from her just a black blood-sucking everything in around her. She rips the oxygen from rooms when she enters. She used a girl named Jennifer's house up the road to fence all her stolen merchandise.

She was involved in the murder of a minor female and the hospitalization of a tv young last in that house, and Jennifer had blonde hair. My sister's partner's ex lives in Princeton harbor on a boat with the ex-convict boyfriend named Jamie of my deceased friend. Who's the end of life hospice and palliative drugs were stolen by your grandson's mom that killed these people, including your grandson. How's that for twisted connections? Wow right?

You'll have to decipher my poor typing. My vision is going quickly. Unfortunately, I have cataracts, and typing with my rheumatoid arthritis is challenging. Suppose there's anything I Can Contribute to your book as far as my experience with the murderess and all she's shared with me and stolen from me. In that case, she's one of the few people I waste energy on hating with a vengeance, but she's so dangerous I can't combat her mano a mano.

I'm glad you are writing a book exposing this vile, diabolical demoness. It will be therapeutic for you as well.

I can't wait to read it. She's a Canadian native Indian with ten children from 8 or 9 different people to collect Native Canadian welfare is the ONLY reason she had these children were as sacrificial lambs now, she receives their death benefits from her tribe. She openly admitted to that as well.

Wow right? She a nasty piece of work, I tell you. I love not letting evil take over.

I tried to take her head off with an ax once. I was so blinded with disgust and fury I lay in wait for her where I was living at the time on Pope Road. It's the only way to defeat the undead and vampires. She is a vampire, a succubus, and a robber of souls. I know I sound crazy as a shit-house rat, so be it, but there are monsters from the legions of darkness, Satan's realm, that walk amongst us living good Christian souls on this earth. They spread disease, corruption, addiction, murder, and all the unclean night that afflicting the weak-willed and those vulnerable lost sheep without strong or without any spiritual connections to their Creator (God) and our Lord and Shepherd Jesus Christ who died for our sins on the cross.

I wasn't successful, but I did scare her, which was even more satisfying because I didn't know that she was capable of fear . . . Ha!

My husband always lets me engage in whatever craziness I feel like conducting, but I tell him I have God. She does not. That is what makes me more powerful in other ways. But she scares me too, and rightfully so. The only person I fear is myself, except her. Her darkness is terrifying because I see her for what she is beneath her disguise of flesh and bone, and it is almost too hideous to behold. I can't look at her for too long, or I'll vomit. I see people as they are inside. I've been given this gift and curse. It is refreshing when I meet beautiful good kind persons that are genuinely made in the image of their Creator.

I know I sound unhinged, but I have experienced things that defy logical explanations. Also, there is another side after the death of the body. The soul lives on, our life force as it is. I have solid proof. My first husband, on his deathbed, told me that he would send me $0.11 every day to let me know he was still watching over me. A penny and a dime, and since 2014, 14 August, I have found a penny and a dime every day, no matter where I may be in Desert Shore Mountain Forest City on my property. It doesn't matter. I have found one every day, and I have jars and jars full of dimes and pennies everywhere and people who hang out with me daily. I tell them about this, and they believe me, but when they witness it with their own eyes, they think there is another side.

Those souls can reach through the veil and touch Our Lives continually and continue to watch over us. After the body is gone, love survives and transcends all people who may die. Still, Love Never Dies, and that is for sure, and I can't wait for the day to come that I can be reunited with all those I've lost that I love so dearly. I don't fear death because I'm comfortable with my relationship with God and my Lord Jesus.

I love you, Uncle, and I wish you success in writing this book. I do.

May God watch over you and protect you.

CHAPTER 9

More Revealed

I am a shape-shift trickster from the Ojibwe Nation. The rats live in the dark. God's children live in the light. God's love was created to love and be loved, not for the unjust and evil.

Severe cancer patients use methadone for the chronic pain that they experience. My mom had broken into a friend of hers home after my mom found out this acquaintance had died of cancer, broke open her drug cabinet, and had taken a bottle of methadone. And she gave it to a friend of mine and said, "Do whatever you want with it, get rid of it".

And in return, the girlfriend of my uncle asked me to try this methadone. I was dead; that $50 bill was taken from me by my uncle. Having no idea of what it was for or the effects led to my murder.

The drug that Sequoyah overdosed on was called methadone. If you suspect someone has overdosed, the most critical step to take is to call 911 so they can receive immediate medical attention.

Once medical personnel arrives, they will administer naloxone if they suspect an opioid drug is involved. These symptoms can be extremely uncomfortable and are why many people find it so difficult to stop. This drug is prescribed for cancer patients in severe pain and near death. Unlike drugs, you can smoke, snort up your nose, are within needle shoot in your arm, and get an instant high. This drug is pill form, liquid, or patch, and from not getting that instant high, they will take more and cross the line, then it is too late.

My uncle tried vaguely to give me mouth-to-mouth resuscitation. They left my body for 16 hours before law enforcement agencies were contacted. And ditch all the paraphernalia and run and make excuses between one another. And especially do not tell the truth. And whatever you do, do not attend the service or give the family Your condolences.

Psalms 104; 29. Thou hides thy face, they are troubled;
now takes away their breath, they die and return to their
dust.

Inspiring, credible, patiently taken out, run like hell.

Monday, 8 PM 20 September 2021. A long-time alcoholic friend walks
in with his dog drunk. The first thing he did was offer me heroin or vodka
with milk. I said neither. So they are all heroin users, and they would lie to
their mothers and sell their mother just for the next high.

And when you get drunk, you say things you should not say, although
he did anyway. Is that what you are doing sitting down here, angry still?
That did it; I said not only that, I got some professionals from Las Vegas
coming out to take care of business. And I said there were ten people
on the list, including the homeowner, my grandson's mother, uncle, and
girlfriend. Then he talked about my grandson's mother, coming in and out
of consciousness and laying on the loveseat with his dog. He came in here
to see what I was doing and pump me for information.

I called him Tuesday, 21 September 2021, at 9 AM. answering machine
said it was full. He called right back drunk or with a real bad hangover upon
hanging up thirty seconds later. I asked him, do you know what spiritual
discernment is? And from being in prison, he had done a lot of reading and
still does. He said not really. It's simple; it just knows the difference between
right and wrong.

Asked him, "do you know what blasphemy of the Holy Spirit is"? He
said yes when you curse out the Holy Spirit, you commit an abomination
against God. No, that's part of it, studying Greek theology. The deeper
meaning of that means that if you know someone is doing wrong, you do
not say anything and let them do it. That is committing blasphemy against
the Holy Spirit, and you will be held responsible for not saying anything.
For this reason, knowing he is a Christian.

I realized that he was not there at the murder scene of my grandson.
He sits in front of the local store every day. And he said, "you know when
those people pull up to the store at the crime scene, they cannot look me in
the eye because of their guilt. And he said, you know, I would kill for you
and do anything for you.

Proverbs 6; 16—19.—"There are six things the Lord hates, seven that are detestable to him. Haughty eyes, a lying tongue, hands that shed innocent blood, a heart that deceives wicked schemes, feet that are quick to rush into evil, a false witness who pours out lies, and a person who stirs up dissension amongst brothers. These are an abomination to the Lord and shall be surely put to death.

And one week before, me being murdered by my mother and friends. A young girl overdosed and died in the same home. One week after being called home, the ambulance was called again to that home.

The mother, the uncle, and girlfriend were at the house the day before, the house owner and her son + others. The one who dialed 911 16 hours later was a young kid, and he was at the service and was shaking with fright. A friend of mine because he was worried and could not find me. **The question is, who told my friend where I was at?**

A guy who lived in Oregon had two broken legs because he was in a motorcycle accident, referred to as "spark plug." Was also at the scene.

And the friend of Sequoyah's was at the scene that night that Grandpa gave a ride with earlier the day previous. Grandpa felt that the overdose was intentional by someone else, and Grandpa's grandson was gullible. Keep in mind the catalyst may have been that Sequoyah could not make change for that $50 bill.

Working hard for tips busing tables to Sequoyah was a lot of money. And being lured into a drug scene with a $50 bill was the demise and murder of Sequoyah.

My mom threatened this lady to keep her mouth shut, and my mom explained exactly what to say to two law enforcement and got a hold of the others, and they started tightening their lying evil ways.

And the detectives questioned the mother and the mother's friend, who initially came to Grandpa's house and informed him of that tragedy. And the detectives said they were both lying. They both said that grandpa was lying. And recorded statements from approximately 20 others. A professional who is patiently going to take care of the sons and daughters of Satan.

Sequoyah, underage, was the youngest member. My mom rented a room from a friend, the homeowner. Being gullible and immature, I was directed to take something others knew they should not have given me. Ten people were having a party in the companionship of my mom and adults, including the homeowner where my mom stayed, who was present at my death and watched me die.

CHAPTER 10

My Grandpa

My grandpa lives by himself in a small town amongst the majestic redwoods of California's Santa Cruz mountains. My grandpa lost his arm to save his soul, and grandpa is in a wheelchair 24 seven. It allows me to help my grandpa with his disabilities/thorns in the flesh. My grandpa is always happy and laughing and has no regrets or resentments.

My grandpa says that his disabilities are his thorns in the flesh that he prayed for either consciously or unconsciously. We always have fun and laugh together.

I had the opportunity to work at a job bussing tables at a busy restaurant on the weekends, 7 miles up a winding mountainous road from grandpa's home.

Grandpa had an extra bedroom for me to stay with him on the weekends. My dad's home and my home, approximately 14 miles opposite grandpa's home, are very secluded, overlooking the Pacific Ocean.

I enjoyed the work, and the town grandpa lives in is a very convenient location with all my friends within walking distance.

Arriving at grandpa's shack every Friday night and stayed with grandpa until my dad came to pick me up on Sunday nights. Grandpa loved the Bible and studying the Bible continuously. I realized that there is a God, Jesus Christ, and the Holy Spirit who lives with grandpa.

Grandpa had one of five prayers we would say upon my arrival at his shack every Friday night. We would hold hands bow our heads, and grandpa would say, listen to the words.

The Our Father. Our father who art in heaven, hallowed be thy name, thy kingdom come thy will be done, on earth as it is in heaven. Give us this day our daily bread, and forgive us our trespasses, as we forgive those who trespass against us. And lead us not into temptation, but deliver us from evil, for thine is the kingdom, power, and glory. Amen.

The Hail Mary. Hail Mary, full of grace, the Lord is with thee, blessed art thou amongst women, and blessed is the fruit of thy womb. Jesus, Holy Mary mother of God, pray for us sinners, now and at the hour of our death. Amen.

The Act Of Contrition. Oh my God, I'm Heartley sorry for ever having offended thee, and I detest all of my sins for thy just punishment. But they have offended thee, my God, who are all good and deserving of all my love. With the help of thy grace, I firmly resolve to sin no more and avoid the near occasions of sin. Amen.

The Apostles Creed. I believe in one God, the Father Almighty, Creator of heaven and earth. I believe in Jesus Christ, His only Son, our Lord, conceived by the Holy Spirit and born of the virgin Mary. He suffered under Pontius Pilate, was crucified, died, and was buried; He descended to hell. On the third day, He rose again from the dead. He ascended to heaven and is seated at the right hand of God the Father almighty. From there, He will come to judge the living and the dead. I believe in the Holy Spirit, the communion of saints, the forgiveness of sins, the body's resurrection, and everlasting life. Amen.

The Serenity Prayer. God, grant me the serenity to accept the things I cannot change. The courage to change the things I can. And the wisdom to know the difference. Amen.

Grandpa also purchased some costly anointing oil from Jerusalem. And gave me a prophetic blessing. Grandpa asked me to put a few drops on his thumb so he could do the sign of the cross on my forehead. I escorted this oil freely up and down my arms, not familiar with the process. And grandpa said, "what are you doing? It's costly!" And we both laughed. One thing about grandpa, when it's over, it is over, and there's no sense crying over spilled milk. You cannot unscramble eggs.

This anointing oil consisted of, Spikenard, Frankincense, Myrrh, Cinnamon, Sandalwood, And Olive Oil.

Grandpa said that the aroma of anointing oils was very pleasing to the Lord. And when you're in the presence of the Holy Spirit, you will smell an odor that you have never smelled before. My dad, grandpa, and I all held hands together and said a prayer a few times.

One day grandpa wanted me to get my driver's license, and I was 16 years old. So getting into grandpas Ford Explorer, we drove around the back way to a small town with curvy roads about 4 miles up and about 7 miles down. I took off fast, and my grandpa said, what are you doing? And I said, "this is how my dad drives."

And grandpa said, "I don't care how your father drives or myself. If you tend to pass a driving test, listen to your grandpa. So in the small town, grandpa was teaching me how it would be with the driving instructor. And on the way back, he said I was perfect. Grandpa did not know that I had driven before, and I was scaring grandpa.

I used to go into my grandpa's bedroom and push on his chest while he was sleeping, bouncing him up and down (that nobody ever attempted to do) and letting grandpa know I was going to a friend's house for a couple of hours and that I would be back. We were both smiling, grandpa always wakes up with a smile on his face, and I always have a smile.

There was a time I had long hair, and I got a haircut and walked into grandpas shack. Grandpa looked at me and was surprised, and grandpa said, you look exactly like I do. And we both smiled and laughed. I love my grandpa, and I am with him at all times, and with grandpa's unshakable faith, he knows that.

My grandpa said to my dad and me, "if I ever kicked the bucket, here is what I would like you to speak at my service, and I will be standing right next to you.

Psalms 23.

(A Psalm of David.) The Lord is my shepherd; I shall not want. He makes me lie down in green pastures; He leads me beside the still waters. He restores my soul; He leads me in the paths of righteousness for His namesake. Though I walk through the valley of the shadow of death, I will fear no evil; for thou art with me; thy rod and staff comfort me. Thou prepares a table before me in the presence of my enemies; thou anoints my head with oil; my cup runs over. Surely goodness and mercy shall follow me all the days of my life, and I will dwell in the house of the Lord forever.

CHAPTER 11

Dimensions of God's love

I am a guardian angel of this family that I love, a compelling divine creation of God. I'm in the presence of all of my immediate family, that love me the most and have shown so much love for me through the grace of God miraculously. My passing and the mourning of family members show that my love will continue in their hearts.

Living here on this earth only in the third dimension, I am in the 11th dimension in heaven. I cannot explain love, joy, and happiness. Remember, you're never alone.

The time in your third earthly dimension is only by the brevity and within a twinkle of an eye. We will all be together again one day, but not yet. Nowhere in the word of God or the Bible does it say to pray for the devil or forgive the devil.

I'm here with my grandpa, whom I love very much. Peace, grace, joy, happiness, protection, guidance, prayers with loving kindness be with all of you through Jesus Christ our Lord's name, amen. God bless with all my love.

It is the year 2021, the year of our Lord Jesus. Christ, not the Dalai Lama, not Mohammed, not the tooth fairy or Mickey Mouse. Professing one of God's elect, we are a divine creation of God. There has never been one of myself, and there will never be another. We should devote our lives to God and service. You can never forget the truth; never remember a lie.

Our faith should be unshakable, and there is no higher than a spiritual high. Greed and lust take, love gives. It's not what you have; it's who you are. God's gift to us is his life; our gift to God is what we do with this life. The only thing we should fear is God our Father and Jesus Christ our Lord. God had to come to this earth in the flesh as Jesus Christ To shed his precious blood on the cross for our wretched sins. Before ascending into heaven, Jesus Christ left us with the Holy Spirit.

Ego (easing God out). BIBLE (basic instruction before leaving earth). There are times we have to admit we are powerless over ourselves, and our lives have become unmanageable. There are times we have to confess our sins, acknowledging to God, ourselves, and another human being the exact nature of our wrongs. Not forsake is to confess your sins and continue doing them. Never to do them again is to admit.

If we seek through prayer and meditation to improve our conscious contact with God as we understand Him, praying only for knowledge of His will for us and the power to carry that out.

No matter how far down the scale we have gone, we will see how our experience can benefit others. That feeling of uselessness and self-pity will disappear. We will lose interest and selfish things and gain interest in our fellows. Self-seeking will slip away. Our whole attitude and outlook on life will change. Fear of people and economic insecurity will leave us. We will intuitively know how to handle situations that used to baffle us. We will suddenly realize that God is doing what we cannot do for ourselves.

It is something fundamental and can get anointed on this undiscovered topic. Manners, yes sir, no sir, please thank you, excuse me, may I pardon me, etc.

This is a prayer of St. Francis of Assisi. Lord, make me an instrument of thy peace! That where there is hatred, I may bring love. That where it is wrong, I may get the spirit of forgiveness. That where there is discord, I may bring harmony. That where there is an error, I may bring truth. That where there is doubt, I may bring faith. That where there is despair, I may bring hope. That where there are shadows, I may bring light. That where there is sadness, I may bring joy. Lord, grant that I may seek rather than comfort, then to be comforted. To understand then to be understood. To love than to be loved. For it is by self-forgetting that one finds. It is by forgiving that one is forgiven. It is by dying that one awakens to eternal life.

That moves throughout the earth, answering prayers and between us to help one another. Children of God walk in the light; sons and daughters of the devil walk in the dark. We will be judged by our thoughts, words, what we do, and what we fail to do. Only a fool would not fear God. God's love and blessings are miraculous; equally so, the wrath of God is hell on earth.

Do not be a doormat and let Satan walk all over you. Blasphemy of the Holy. Spirit is the only unforgiven sin. And that is when someone is doing wrong, and you have spiritual discernment (knowing the difference between right and wrong), and you do not say anything to that person committing a sin or doing something wrong.

That is blasphemy of the Holy Spirit, and you will be judged accordingly. God's will be done, not ours. Sitting by and letting evil control your life, you can count on a trip to hell. Two things are guaranteed, we are all going to kick the bucket, and we are all going to stand before Jesus Christ, our Lord, for judgment. So please do not stand around pretending you are born with brain damage and walking around brain dead, pretending you are holier than thou; a hypocrite in the Bible can count on a trip to hell.

When you are wrong, do the searching and moral inventory of yourself and promptly admit it. And make amends, only accept when to do so would injure them or others.

Matthew 12; 31.—Wherefore I say unto you, All manner of sin and blasphemy shall be forgiven unto men: but the blasphemy against the Holy Ghost shall not be forgiven unto men. Proverbs 6; 23 For the commandment is a lamp, and the law is light; and reproofs of instruction are the way of life:

CHAPTER 12

Eternity Together Faith Believing

My grandpa's faith is unshakable, experiencing a lifetime of miracles with his spiritual eyes wide open, walking by faith, not by sight. There is a reason for everything, and as you read, the miracles will be revealed to you later in life. Why do bad things happen to good people? Because God loves us that much. Occasionally, God will stick us into the fire to burn the impurities from this precious piece of gold, "our soul." After we are placed in the fire enough, we get the wisdom through the Holy Spirit, devoting our lives to God and service, helping others to the gates of heaven.

Through the grace of Jesus Christ our Lord, My grandpa's miracles cannot be explained or written beyond my grandpa's comprehension or imagination. Having faith, believing in the word of God, Bible, where angels are mentioned from Genesis throughout the Bible to Revelation. Angels are mentioned 105 times in the Old Testament, 185 times in the New Testament, Hebrews 13; 2.—Be not forgetful to entertain strangers, for thereby some have entertained angels unawares. Sequoyah Hunter, God's Soul Hunter, is a shape-shift trickster from the Ojibwe Nation.

God willing, we will help others lighten their loads every chance we have. Grandpa is writing from the heart and soul, letting the Spirit of God flow through him because it brings joy to undiscovered dreams. Grandpa humbles himself before God and gives Him thanks and appreciation of understanding. "Let there be few spaces in our togetherness and let the winds of the heavens dance between us. Love one another but make not a burden of love: It is quiet when the spirit moves you; it will be well worth the adventure if you decide to venture into the dream one day."

We have lessons to learn and teach one another; it is a blessing in disguise. Being granted more grace from God in a lifetime than most people think about or are even aware exists. God is grandpa's spiritual soul mate through Jesus Christ our Lord, and if all my grandpa does is God's will to help others, grandpa's future is living at the head of the dream, one moment at a time, and loving God, who is the keeper of his soul and spirit. If we love this life and all the worldly amenities, we don't love God. You must have absolute faith to be living our calling.

May our love never come apart, incredibly straight from the heart! May you always have a rainbow of smiles on your faces and in your hearts forever and ever! Eventually, we will understand that love is more than verses on Valentine's and romance in the movies. We will begin to know that love is here and now, honest and true, and the most valuable thing—for love is the creator of our favorite memories and the foundation of our fondest dreams.

Love is a commitment that should always be cherished with reverence, a fortune that can never be spent, and a seed that can grow even in the most unlikely places. This mysterious and magical joy, a radiance that never fades, is the greatest treasure of all - only known to those who love. Give the courage to be an imperfect friend who genuinely cares, and then discover that there is a God. We need not be consumed by guilt for failure to achieve His likeness and image by the one who sent an Angel. Progress is our goal, and His perfection is the beacon, light-years away, that draws us on. The joy is in the footsteps, so enjoy the ride.

CHAPTER 13

Proof that God exists

You say, "Yes, I'm willing," but am I too consigned to a life where I shall be stupid, mundane, and glum, like some righteous people? I know I must get along without love, but how? Have you a sufficient substitute? Yes, there is a replacement; it is exceedingly more than that. It is a friendly Angel who honestly cares. With your imagination fired, you will find freedom from care, boredom, and worry. Life will mean something at last. Joy and liberty are not stations we arrive at; they are a way of traveling. The most gratifying years of your existence lie ahead. Joyfully, we find friends, and you will see them as well.

Let it begin with me. The distance is nothing if, even for a moment, we cross paths along our travels that make a difference. It is only the first step toward COURAGE that is difficult. There is a "spiritual side" to love; the love of one who cares is spiritual.

Some of the evidence of a spiritual awakening is maturity and an end to habitual hatred. Love each other, be passionately loved in return, and believe and trust with honesty, without understanding. That something lets the sunrise in the morning and set at night, makes the flowers in the spring, drops in the fall, and gives the birds song.

Imagine that we can be possessively loving of a few, ignore the many, and continue to envy or hate anybody, has to be abandoned, if only a little at a time. We can try to stop controlling, unreasonable demands upon those we love. We can show kindness where we had shown none. We can practice justice and courtesy with those we dislike and perhaps go out of the way to understand and help them. Courtesy, kindness, justice, and love are the keynotes by which we can achieve harmony with practically anybody.

My grandpa lost his arm to save his soul.

The answer to his prayer. Matthew 5; 30.—"And if thy right hand offend thee, cut, and cast it from thee; for it is profitable for thee that one of thy members should perish, and not that thy whole body should be cast into hell."

Working in the woods logging with his brother (my uncle Tom), a widow-maker hit my grandpa in the back and severed the five nerves from the spine going to his left arm. My grandpa looked up to heaven with tears pouring down his cheeks and said, "thank you, God." My grandpa could not have thought of a better answer to his prayer. He was getting ready to purchase another Harley-Davidson motorcycle. Losing that arm saved my grandpa's soul. My grandpa thanks God that God, through a supernatural prayer, had taken grandpa's left arm and not his right arm. My grandpa's soul's journey. Or these words written down would not be here to read.

My great-grandpa (my grandpa's dad)

My grandpa witnessed a conversation that his dad, my great-grandpa, said. My great-grandpa received a telephone call from his brother in Washington. His mother had just slipped into a coma, and my great-grandpa should fly from California to Washington State to see his mother for the last time. My great-great-grandma was in the hospital. When my great-grandpa walked into the room, my great-great-grandma woke up from her coma, then asked my great-grandpa, "how are the children doing, Gene"? My great-grandpa said, fine, mom". She then went back into her coma and died.

God called my grandpa on the telephone

Grandpa found out that drugs and alcohol were a springboard for evil. Spirits to come on in and take control of his mind, body, personality, and actions. He never knew who he was until July 19th, 2002, when he had a spiritual awakening, which catapulted him into the fourth dimension of understanding the purpose in life.

As a witness to my grandpa's encounter with the Holy Spirit, my grandpa was sitting in his office after his third wife edges left him, with a bottle of

151 Bacardi, and a little Kahlúa and cream, with a gram of speed placed into the drink.

My grandpa had this supernatural thought, seeing no light at the end of the tunnel for him ever quitting drugs or alcohol. "God, please help me. I do not know how to stop." At that thought, the phone rang, and it was a friend of my great grandpa's who had 43 years of sobriety in the Alcoholics Anonymous program, who never called my grandpa. And just like my grandpa, how was he doing? My grandpa said, "one minute, please, I will be right back. The mental obsession and the physical compulsion instantly left my grandpa at that moment. He put down the phone, went and flushed, and dumped everything he could find. I returned to the phone and said, much better now, "Carl." My grandpa checked himself into the Kaiser chemical dependency program and the Veterans Administration program and absorbed himself in three Alcoholics Anonymous meetings a day. This was July 19th, 2002, and my grandpa never looked back. Grandpa quit dancing with the devil. He did not tiptoe around hell; he danced right through the middle, doing a little soft shoe, doing the Boogaloo, trip to the light fantastic, spun the devil around, bid him farewell, and never looked back.

My grandpa sits in a wheelchair 24 hours a day. Although he can drive a vehicle and has his driver's license, he can take a shower, and he cooks for himself, except when I had the opportunity to bring my grandpa home meals from the restaurant where I worked. My grandpa works out, watches evangelist programs (Billy Graham, etc.), fasts and prayer, and writes and reads the Bible continuously. And my grandpa is happier than a clam at high tide.

Because he has the joy of the Lord and the Holy Spirit and knows without a doubt with his unshakable faith that he will be in heaven with me one day, the miracle is that everything happens for a reason; nothing happens perchance. My grandpa writes these words with the faith and understanding that others may have the opportunity to read these words. Miraculously through the grace of God, the brevity of life is all too short.

Angel preventing rape and possibly murder?

My grandpa lived next to a widowed lady who had two sons and a young daughter. They lived next to one another in a recreational vehicle park. Her daughter attended high school locally in the area. One warm summer evening, at 3 AM, for some Godly reason, getting out of bed only wearing underwear and sitting outside on the front porch to have a cigarette; when all of a sudden observed a young girl running as fast as she could down the driveway—appearing that she was running toward the neighbor's trailer. In a small vehicle, behind her was a guy trying to chase her down and catch her. He noticed grandpa sitting on a hard redwood bench on the front porch. This guy asked my grandpa if he had seen a girl running down the driveway?" Informed him sternly a USMC command voice to get off the property or would call 911. He looked at my grandpa and drove off as fast as possible. The next day, the neighbor told a story about a guy who had pulled into our area. He had held an underage girl against her will at gunpoint and raped her repeatedly for two days. This young girl was a friend of her daughter. She was able to get out of the car in front of the park, run and hide behind one of the work trucks.

My grandpa imagined at the time that the fleeing girl had been her daughter, who fought with one of her boyfriends.

Not realizing the situation until the next day when the lady came over to the trailer, explained the case, and mentioned that that was real.

Never before or since getting out of bed at 3 AM to have a cigarette and sit outside in underwear on the front porch.

Faithfully thanked God through the Holy Spirit for this night, guided to a place grandpa needed to be.

The authorities did catch this sick individual, assuming that he is still in prison today. You figure it out—waking at just that moment coincidence, luck, or the Lord through the Holy Spirit, who sent an angel to wake up my grandpa?

My great uncle Tom killed and spiritually came to my grandpa.

And from the dimension where I am in heaven, the foresight cannot be explained or written into words, with the Holy Spirit working through grandpa writing these words, coming from myself, Sequoyah Hunter.

When losing a close loved one, say a little prayer with unshakable faith, "God, please give a sign that a loved one is okay." Saying a prayer the night that grandpa's brother (uncle Tom) was killed riding a Harley-Davidson motorcycle going to a recovery meeting when a deer jumped out in front of him.

The following day, at about 7:30 AM, grandpa heard his brother enter grandpa's home as the front door slid open. He was talking to the cat (Arnold), as usual. Grandpa's brother fixed himself some breakfast, and grandpa smelled the aroma of bacon. Then grandpa heard his brother speaking to the cat, then listened to the door slide closed, wide-awake, and not dreaming. Grandpa usually asks his brother, what's going on?" But that particular morning, grandpa said nothing. He just wanted to relish and acknowledge his words and the miracle. God sends us right back here—to guide, protect, and love the ones we care about the most.

The day before my grandpa's brother's service, grandpa's caretaker came in to get him ready, as usual, and said, "I'm not sure if I was dreaming or if it happened." "What are you talking about?" Asking him, he explained to me that your brother had opened his door, as he had done every morning (—the caretaker lives in a guesthouse next to grandpa—), and grandpa's brother had said, "Let's go. It's time to get up!" Grandpa's brother would slam his door closed and then open it again and ask him for a cigarette on a typical day. The day grandpa's brother got called home, he quit smoking cigarettes.

Grandpa's brother avoided flying on airplanes or taking elevators; he feared the motion of rising and falling. After his funeral service, my aunt Kathy from Los Angeles decided to take her nieces and nephew shopping for items of their choice. Her two sisters went along with the grandchildren and grandpa's brother and daughter. They all got on the elevator; the elevator stopped in between floors. They said they were in the elevator for about forty-five minutes until the technicians let them out of the elevator.

Are these just mere coincidences? Maybe they just happened for a reason. Believing it was grandpa's brother's spirit—just God answering our prayers, let us know that Tom is okay and in a safe place. About a week and a half after the service, a good friend of my grandpa's brother and a handyman came into grandpa's house. And said he'd had the weirdest dream and that he had to tell me about his plan.

A friend of my grandpa's brother had ridden in his truck and left his cell phone there. Forgetting to get the phone, he called him and said he must have left his phone in the pickup truck. He looked in his truck and could not find it. That night, he went to bed, and he had a dream. My grandpa's brother came to him in his dream and said, "Look under the truck seat. The phone will be wrapped in a plastic bag; you will find your phone." He did not think much about it, but he looked under the truck's seat out of curiosity. There, under the seat, was the phone wrapped in a plastic bag.

We are only in the third dimension, and in his flaming chariot, God brought Isaac through eleven dimensions to the height of heaven. After my grandpa's brother was taken home to heaven. Grandpa attended a recovery meeting. Five or six men came to him after the session and informed him that they would not be sober today if it were not for grandpa's brother. They wanted to thank grandpa and give their condolences to the family.

Lacey called on Jesus to prevent evil possession from raping her.

My grandpa was good friends with the lady he met in the program Alcoholics Anonymous, and her name is Lacey, from the upper state of New York. Lacey mentioned a fascinating story to my grandpa at one time; she likes to keep in shape by jogging and to run. She decided to take a run one day, and she mentioned that there was a force field that held her back, telling her not to go on this run. It was a rural trail going through the woods. Not many people use it, and she remembered some guy had jogged past her with a dog. The dog barked at her twice, and she felt the dog was telling her not to go on this run.

Without realizing the signs until after, she started jogging on this trail, and she said, this nice-looking good-looking gentleman jogging towards her, and they both smiled at each other. About 20 feet from each other, and then for no reason at all, this guy grabbed her twister thumbs behind her back, ripped at her shirt, and intended to rape her, and Lacey felt that this guy could have killed her easily. Lacey yelled at the top of her lungs, Jesus, PLEASE HELP. She did not know she could scream that loud.

Immediately, this evil-possessed guy let go of her, dropped to the ground on all fours, slithered away from her like an animal, and looked back at her as he slithered away.

Who wakes up on a slab in the hospital morgue and starts walking?

My cousin Samuel who lives in Alaska, mentioned to my grandpa one day, as my grandpa witnessed what he was hearing, in almost a state of disbelief. A friend of my cousin Samuel is from Alaska and Inuit (Eskimo/ Native American). And this friend of my cousin Samuels is renting a room from Samuel. My cousin, Samuel, asked my grandpa, 'have or heard of the word Tartarus'? Only mentioned once in the Bible, It is the lowest level of hell, where you are frozen under ice or half out of the ice, for eternity, alive.

My cousin Samuel had gotten drunk and started stabbing himself with a knife in the stomach while fighting with his girlfriend. They medevac him from the island he was on to a medical center. When he was pronounced dead, they placed him on the slab in the morgue before embalming and getting his body ready for burial.

He woke up and walked out of the morgue, startling everyone who had seen him, that pronounced him dead. He said, "it was the evilest, cold, dark, dreary, and is a very eerie feeling." Grandpa did not believe my cousin Samuel when he told my grandpa about this incident and wanted to talk specifically with that gentleman.

My cousin Samuel said, "okay." And call my grandpa back when he got home from work. My grandpa talked with this gentleman extensively about what happened. And it was just like my cousin Samuel said.

Anyway, this gentleman is scared to death because he does not want to go back to that place.

An Angel came to a renowned neurosurgeon's home.

An actual incident my grandpa witnessed while watching his favorite evangelist, "Billy Graham." Billy Graham had mentioned this story is in Reader's Digest.

It was a snowy, cold, windy winter evening when a neurosurgeon heard a knock on his door. When he opened the door, there stood a little girl, 11 years old, and asked this famous neurosurgeon if he could please come to her home and help her mother because she was sick. The neurosurgeon does not make house calls. Looking into the little girl's eyes, there was something about her, and he said, "okay ." As he grabbed his coat and hat.

The doctor followed her to her home, and when the doctor observed the mother, he knew instantly she would not have made it through the night without medical attention. He immediately called the ambulance. The doctor then said to the lady, "your daughter is a beautiful little girl ." And the lady said, "what little girl? My daughter died one month ago. You can look in the closet where her clothes are hanging." The doctor went over and opened the closet door, and there were the same little coat, dress, and shoes the little girl had on when she came to his home.

Wake up from a coma to make amends

It was 20 years ago, and my last wife cheated on me. I was on drugs and alcohol when I met her. Isn't it funny that I've been clean and sober for 20 years I live alone? Anyway, we always remained friends. I was her fifth husband. And you might say I let her take me to the cleaners. She spent thousands of dollars on horses, horse trailers, and trucks. And I was a hard worker who made a lot of money a year. And she got married two more times after me. And I remain friends with her, not just her but her father I liked.

I call myself the nickel because I was number five. I called her seventh husband lucky. Anyway, her daughter called me one day and said that if I wanted to see her mother, I better come to her home, where her mother was in a coma as soon as I walked in the door of her daughter's home up by Sacramento. She came out of her coma, and we conversed for about an hour. She had some rare genetic disease. And she made amends to me about all the money she had spent.

And I said, "you can't unscramble eggs and we cannot cry over spilled milk. everything's okay, and it's over". Anyway, as soon as I left her daughter's home, she went back into a coma and passed on.

Shape-Shift

Shape-Shifting is not a rare phenomenon but keeps occurring around my family. Native American tradition, especially from my Ojibway Nation, I am a free spirit.

My dad was driving along the highway in his pickup truck and shape-shifting into a mountain lion. Just standing there watching my dad slowly drive-by as he looked at me.

My dad was driving down our long r ural driveway, and I shape-shifted into a mountain lion, slowly running alongside my dad's truck and then running slightly in front of him. Looking back at my dad until my dad knew it was me taunting him and letting him know I was okay.

The day before I was scheduled to graduate high school, I was found as a mountain lion in the English classroom. They close the small high school down for the day. And I would not leave until I made national news.

My dad owns a tree service, and as he removed a tree, I shape-shifted into a bird and stayed in the nest, looking at my dad.

My auntie, who lives in Los Angeles, was jogging with her dog when I shape-shifted into a bird and kept landing in front of her and circling. My auntie could have reached out and touched me. Then I thought I would fly into her head and circle her. My name is Sequoyah Hunter, I am a shape-shift trickster, and I come to my family with loving guidance.

CHAPTER 14

God's Messenger "Soul Hunter"

This is how I, "Sequoyah Hunter," lived my short life before I was deprived of fulfilling God's calling.

Give it all away to keep it. Worry is the opposite of faith. Pray together for friendship and continuously reinvent our relationship to growth, truth, honesty, freedom, fun, enjoyment, love, and strength. ***Psalms 91; 11. "For He will command His angels concerning you, to guard you in all your ways"***

My spirit was in my room at grandpa's

I did not want to leave because I loved my grandpa and dad so much. I could get back into my grandpa's house into my room, where it was safe. My body died at 2 AM; my spirit was in grandpa's home in my bedroom when grandpa thought I was home. And those are the noises grandpa heard, thinking that I was home. Spiritually I was in my room at Grandpa's while my body was in that drug house.

Grandpa then went to sleep and did not get up until late the next day, about 4 PM. He was starting to get a little concerned about the whereabouts of his grandson. Although Grandpa, Hearing noises coming from Sequoyah's room from time to time. It just seemed a little strange. Grandpa thought he might have had a friend over in his room.

Grandpa felt that the noises coming from Sequoyah's room were Sequoyah's spirit.

Sequoyah did not want to leave his present life and fought to be with my dad, family, friends, and grandpa. Sequoyah was letting grandpa know supernaturally that it was not my time yet. However, God sent the Angels finally to take Sequoyah home to heaven.

In the tragedy of being murdered, we die for our sins, when Sequoyah was scared to death to leave what he had loved the most. His dad, grandpa, and his family and good friends.

My mother and uncle walked around my body while I was dying, the entire time before I finally succumbed to the drugs that murdered me. My heart was broken that they would not help me. When I could no longer hold on, I went to the safest place spiritually was in my room at my grandpa's home. I finished my battle of fighting to stay until God sent angels to come and finally take me to heaven.

They should have saved my life; with their thinking impaired and worried about themselves, and they watched me die as I was begging for help.

And did not have the common courtesy even to dial 911, and the Sheriff's Department did not do a DNA test on his lips of Sequoyah to see if anyone had given him mouth-to-mouth resuscitation. My uncle tried to give me mouth-to-mouth resuscitation.

The sheriff's department also interviewed 40 people about this incident. Why did they not go to grandpa's house and investigate the last place where Sequoyah was staying at the time of the murder? Being an angel sent from God to care for and protect the just and bring down the evil and unjust. I am a "Soul Hunter," Sequoyah Hunter Klingele. God's love is equivalent to God's wrath.

Sequoyah, let's grandpa know supernaturally.

My grandpa, I love very much. My grandpa has a costly printer with five ink tanks. My grandpa was printing out a picture of me playing ice hockey that my dad had taken at a playoff game for the state championship.

Picture of Sequoyah#84 black and white professional
ice hockey stance my dad had taken of me

The image my grandpa was printing out was in black-and-white. And grandpa's caretaker was with my grandpa at the time. When my grandpa printed the picture out, I wanted it in a stunning aqua ice blue that made it more authentic looking. So I supernaturally fixed my grandpa's printer to where it would print out my picture the way I wanted it.

Picture of the Sequoyah aqua ice blue. Sequoyah#84 supernaturally
and miraculously printed this picture, this is the color I
liked, that no camera or Photoshop could duplicate

The following image my grandpa printed was smeared with different color inks. My grandpa then printed out two more shots on photo paper.

That printed out smeared ink smudges. My grandpa did not know that I was right there orchestrating the printing of my picture and only my image the way I wanted it. My grandpa and his caretaker Jerry worked on grandpa's printer for about 1/2 hour, thinking it was just the magenta ink. My grandpa ended up changing all five ink tanks on his printer. And finally, I do grandpa get back to work. Grandpa smiled, and he knew instantly with his unshakable faith that it was me, his grandson Sequoyah. Grandpa looked up with a big smile, knowing that I was right there orchestrating the procedure of my picture being printed. And I smile back.

And I made sure there was a witness of God's love shining supernaturally with the Holy Spirit working through my grandpa. With my grandpa's caretaker, Jerry, listening to what my grandpa said, my grandpa knew that it was me. There is no way any photo editor would have duplicated the color I wanted for my picture.

The dimension of love that God has cannot be explained; I can be everywhere and with everyone; at the same time, I care to be with others because I am a soul hunter for the just and the unjust.

Every time grandpa tells anyone of the experience my dad and my grandpa had together, they should not have gone through, although thank God they were together when my dad went into that home where my mom was staying to identify my body. Tears come from my grandpa's eyes of love when telling the story to others.

Anonymous friend of grandpa's

My grandpa is chatting online with a friend I like; she is a beautiful young lady, and I know my grandpa cares for her; they talk on messenger. And my grandpa was telling her the story about how the evil forces tragically took his grandson. This lady friend of my grandpa was very interested in knowing everything about the details, and tears of joy started flowing from my grandpa's eyes. And my grandpa was sending his friend pictures of me and the service and me playing ice hockey and my dad and my aunt.

And grandpa was tired of sending pictures of this tragedy that happened. My grandpa was getting exhausted. It took quite a while to download each picture on messenger to send to his friend.

So I had to take charge and start downloading images that I wanted grandpa's friend to see.

So when grandpa thought he was finished downloading pictures, it was time for me to take over. I started downloading photo after picture of myself that I thought my grandpa would have wanted her to see. My grandpa could not figure it out right away, and it seemed to him like his computer was messing up.

However, my grandpa knew that his computer could not download pictures that fast. And suddenly, my grandpa knew that it was me. And my grandpa instantly told his friend, you're just witnessing a miracle. My grandson is here with us right now, and he is condoning our friendship for one another.

I let Grandpa's friend know that I liked her because she liked my grandpa. And they could not stop talking or chatting back and forth on messenger about this incident. My grandpa said, my grandson introduced himself to you.

Two days later, they were chatting again on messenger. And this friend of my grandpa said that she had a dream about Hunter. She always calls me "Hunter." She said she was walking to the store when two men came out and tried to jump her and that Hunter showed up with the baseball bat and chased them away. And what my grandpa knew instantly with his unshakable faith that I was in grandpa's friend's dream, and this happened. So please do not worry or stress.

CHAPTER 15

Angel Assignment "Soul Hunter"

"Soul Hunter". The word angel means "messenger." God is able to send angels to aid anyone on earth at any time as He works out His plan of salvation for humanity. God's word reveals that angels have differing levels of responsibility and honor. The majority of biblical references to angelic encounters with humans show angels appearing in the form of a man. This explains how some humans have "unwittingly entertained angels" (Hebrews 13:2).

In Matthew 18:10, we read of angels watching over God's "little ones"—meaning those who become childlike in Christ (verses 3-4). While angels are charged with protecting God's faithful people on earth (Psalms 34:7; 91:11), the popular concept of a specific guardian angel being assigned to every individual—whether they follow Christ or not—is not supported in the Bible.

When angels appeared to people outside of a dream or vision, they came in the appearance of a man. In this manner, angels spoke face-to-face with God's faithful servants, including Abraham (Genesis 18:2), Lot (Genesis 19:15), Jacob (Genesis 32:1), David (2 Samuel 24:17), Peter (Acts 12:7), Paul (Acts 27:23), Mary (Luke 1:28), a group of shepherds (Luke 2:13), the women at Christ's tomb (Matthew 28:2-5) and numerous others (Hebrews 13:2).

On other occasions, angels appeared in dreams or visions (Genesis 28:12; Matthew 1:20; Acts 10:3). Those encounters were just as vivid and real as if the person were fully awake and holding a conversation with the angel (Acts 12:9).

God created angels (Psalms 33:6; 148:2-5). They exist in the nonphysical spirit realm and are called "ministering spirits" (Hebrews 1:14). God's faithful angels are called holy and elect (Matthew 25:31; 1 Timothy 5:21).

Angels are described as being "greater in power and might" than humans (2 Peter 2:11). Considering this point, the psalmist says of man, "For You have made him a little lower than the angels" (Psalm 8:5). But in the world to come, humans who become part of the Kingdom of God will have authority over the angels (1 Corinthians 6:3; Hebrews 2:5-8).

Angels were created to be God's servants, messengers, and representatives in His universe-ruling government. Angels are commissioned to minister to the Spirit-begotten children of God as "fellow servants" of those who are His spiritual heirs (Hebrews 1:14; Revelation 19:10).

Humanity's destiny is not limited to the physical realm. God designed us to transcend the glory of the angels and even rule over them. If we wish to be a part of God's grand plan, we must prepare our hearts now.

Some of the future roles for angels have been revealed to us in God's Word. God's holy angels are prophesied to accompany Jesus Christ during His triumphant return to earth (Matthew 16:27; 25:31). They will also assist Christ in separating the righteous from the wicked (Matthew 13:39, 41, 49).

CHAPTER 16

Hockey Friends
Welcomed Sequoyah Hunter

Tuesday, a hockey team is waiting for Sequoyah.

Virtual tribute planned to honor Humboldt Broncos bus crash victims.

Tuesday marks the third anniversary of the deadly bus accident.

On June 19th, 2018, members of the Humboldt Broncos hockey team attended a news conference in Las Vegas months after that community was devastated by the junior Broncos bus crash that killed 16.

Posted at 10:43 AM, April 6th, 2021, and last updated at 9:43 AM, April 6th, 2021. On Tuesday, a virtual tribute is planned to honor the 16 Humboldt Broncos junior hockey team members who died three years ago in a bus crash.

On April 6th, 2018, the deadly accident occurred when the bus carrying the Canadian junior hockey team was struck by a semi-trailer that ran a stop sign.

On Monday, the NHL reported that the City of Humboldt and the Humboldt Broncos Memorials Committee announced a Broncos tribute center and a roadside memorial at the bus crash site.

In a statement, Prime Minister Justin Trudeau said that Tuesday, "we remember those taken from us far too soon."

"We also hold in our thoughts their loved ones and everyone whose lives were forever changed that tragic day," Trudeau said. "We mourn with them as they continue to work through their pain, anger, and grief."

A Saskatchewan city says it has a plan to commemorate the deadly Broncos bus crash permanently.

The announcement by the City of Humboldt came on the eve of the third anniversary of the crash, which claimed the lives of 16 people and injured 13 others on April 6th, 2018.

Leave a Stick Out By The Door for Sequoyah Hunter - Memorial Tribute

@SequoyahKlingele
Most Popular Jay Smith—stick out by the door (for Sequoyah)
Jay Smith - Stick Out By The Door (For Sequoyah)

On April 6th, 2018, a coach bus collided with a semi-truck just north of Saskatchewan, Canada killing 16 people and injuring 13. The bus carried members of the Humboldt Broncos Jr. Ice Hockey team and coaches, and others associated with the team.

On April 6th, 2021, the Humboldt Broncos recruited Sequoyah Hunter, a Jr. Roller and Ice Hockey Champion from California, to heaven to play hockey using the clouds as their rink.

Famous Canadian Country music star Jay Smith, also known as Smitty Kingston, wrote a tribute song for the Humboldt Broncos called Stick Out By The Door (Humboldt Strong) that instantly went viral with millions of people streaming it. When Jay heard about Sequoyah's story, he graciously dedicated a personal message and version of the song to Sequoyah, his father, and the Coastside Cougars.

We are asking everybody to please go to this tribute Facebook page tonight and post a picture of your "light on and stick out by the door" (or anything you want to share if you do not have a hockey stick) and a message for Sequoia. You can also see the video of Jay Smith personally singing the song to Sequoia and Kenny. We know Sequoia is up there in heaven, slapping some major hockey pucks and the humble Broncos right by his side.

His father, Kenny, and Kenny's sister Kathy, including sequoias hockey teammates and coaches. Waiting patiently, one day they will all be together.

Stick out by the door" by J Smith, dedicated to Sequoia Hunter, Kenny's father, and his coast side hockey teammates and coaches. Also, the black star ice hockey team. And coaches.

We left our sticks out at the rink and signed all our names with the plans for you to sit on, just in case you wanted one more game; there are no referees or scoreboards. Use the clouds as a hockey ring while playing with all your friends. All the hotel hallway games were played or slap shots on the bus. There wasn't anything in this world that meant this much to us, and we will use the tears to flood the rink and your prayers to keep us warm. This won't be our last game. Yeah, we are still cougar strong. Hey, dad, well, I made it to the show; you always tell me that I would, so don't worry anymore. I've got my teammates by my side, so you don't have to cry. Just promise me one last thing you will leave the light on and put my stick out by the door.

You can also use the hashtag -
#LeaveAStickOutByTheDoorForSequoyah—Jay Smith (Smitty Kingston) can be found at
https://open.spotify.com/artist/6gnpwxIEBphNRfQrAS2lvu

All Videos
0:53
The Enforcer - 5/31/2019
Six days ago
Jay Smith - Stick Out By The Door (For Sequoyah)
Six days ago

Sequoyah Hunter is in the Big League
When he was a kid, he'd be up at five
Take shots 'til eight and make the thing drive
Out after school and back on ice
That was his life, and he was going to play in the big league
The big league

Not many ways out of this cold small town
You work in the trees and get laid on the ground
And if you're going to jump, it will be with the game
Real fast and tough is the only clear lane to the big league

My boy's going to play in the big league
My boy's going to turn some heads
My boy's going to play in the big league
My boy's going to knock 'em dead
The big league

All the right moves when he turned sixteen
Out with his friends at the lake in La Honda
Just when I needed of of you the most
You ran and left me alone in that house
To the big league

My boy's going to play in the big league
My boy's going to turn some heads
My boy's going to play in the big league
My boy's going to knock 'em dead

Heaven's Gates, Hockey Friends Welcomed Sequoyah Hunter.

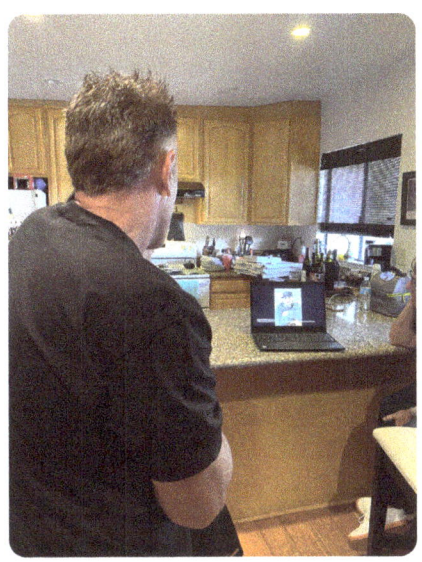

My Dad Video Chatting With Country-Western
Singer-Songwriter From Canada Jay Smith
Does Not Like The Changes Songs From The Original One He Had Written
Leave A Light On And Put A Stick Out By The Door
For A Busload Of Canadian Ice Hockey Players Who Were
Killed Three Years Exactly The Same Day, I Was Murdered

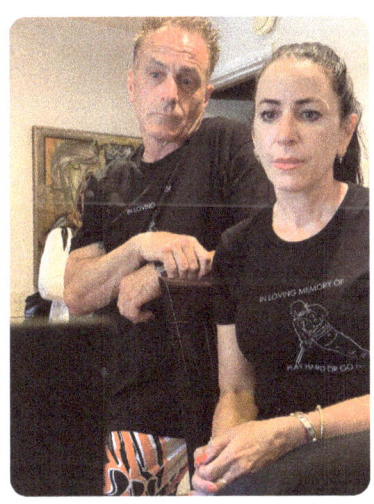

My Dad And My Auntie Kathy Video Chatting Live
With Country Western Singer From Canada
Jay Smith At My Dad's Home And My Home

Jay Smith Personally Knows The Best Ice Hockey Players In Canada
Tried Himself To Play A Little Ice Hockey Back In The
Day And Found Out After Being A Goalie
His Calling Was The Guitar And Singing
Change The Lyrics Of The Original Song For Me Sequoyah Hunter
(Soul Hunter) Just For My Dad And My Auntie Kathy

Leave a Stick Out By The Door for Sequoyah Klingele - Memorial Tribute

@SequoyahKlingele

Most Popular

Jay Smith - Stick Out By The Door (For Sequoyah)
On April 6th 2018, a coach bus collided with a semitruck just north of Saskatchewan, Canada killing 16 people and injuring 13. The bus was carrying members of the Humboldt Broncos Jr. Ice Hockey team as well as coaches an others associated with the team. Exactly 3 years later to the day on April 6th 2021, the Humboldt Broncos recruited Sequoyah Hunter Klingele, a Jr. Roller and Ice Hockey Champion from Half Moon Bay California, to Heaven to play hockey with them using the clouds as their rink. Famous Canadian Country music star Jay Smith, or also known as Smitty Kingston, wrote a tribute song for the Humboldt Broncos called Stick Out By The Door (Humboldt Strong) that instantly went viral with millions of people streaming it. When Jay heard about Sequoyah's story, he graciously dedicated a personal message and version of the song to Sequoyah, his father Kenny, and the Coastside Cougars. We ask of you to please leave your hockey stick (or anything you want) out by the door with the light on in remembrance of Sequoyah and post a picture to our page. You can also use the hashtag - #LeaveAStickOutByTheDoorForSequoyah ------------------------------- Jay Smith (Smitty Kingston) can be found at https://open.spotify.com/artist/6gnpwxIEBphNRfQrAS2lvu

All Videos

0:53
The Enforcer - 5/31/2019
6 days ago

Jay Smith - Stick Out By The Door (For Sequoyah)
6 days ago

Mr. Smith Is A Great Man And Look Forward
To One Day Meeting My Dad
He gave All His Compassion And Condolences For All
Of My Hockey Friends, Fans, And Family

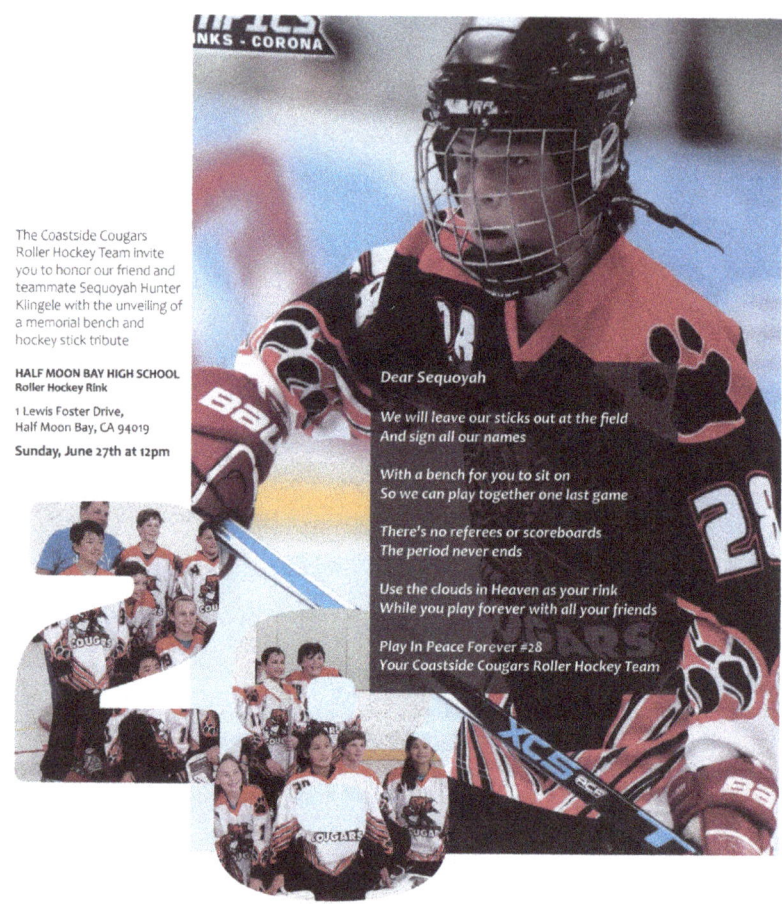

The Coastside Cougars Roller Hockey Team invite you to honor our friend and teammate Sequoyah Hunter Klingele with the unveiling of a memorial bench and hockey stick tribute

HALF MOON BAY HIGH SCHOOL
Roller Hockey Rink

1 Lewis Foster Drive,
Half Moon Bay, CA 94019

Sunday, June 27th at 12pm

Dear Sequoyah

We will leave our sticks out at the field
And sign all our names

With a bench for you to sit on
So we can play together one last game

There's no referees or scoreboards
The period never ends

Use the clouds in Heaven as your rink
While you play forever with all your friends

Play In Peace Forever #28
Your Coastside Cougars Roller Hockey Team

A special thank you to the following who donated time and resources to make this possible:

GoFundMe Fundraiser Team (Sequoyah's Seacrest Friends) Marina Pokorny and her Dad Stephen Pokorny, Renee Casentini, Mayah Johnson, Sadie Nolan, Emma Steadman and Ashley Grant

Smith Steelworks (memorial bench design and fabrication)
Instant Display Cases
Half Moon Bay Building and Garden
Coach Mark Modena and Family

A dedication picture for all my teammates. I will be waiting for patiently in heaven where we will play hockey on the clouds

70

LEAVE A LIGHT ON AND PUT A STICK OUT BY THE DOOR FOR SEQUOYAH

On **April 6th 2018** a coach bus collided with a semitruck just north of Saskatchewan Canada killing 16 people and injuring 13. The bus was carrying members of the Humboldt Broncos Jr. Ice Hockey team as well as coaches and others associated with the team.

Exactly 3 years later to the day on **April 6th 2021** the Humboldt Broncos recruited 16 year old Sequoyah Hunter Klingele, a Jr. Roller and Ice Hockey Champion from Half Moon Bay California, to Heaven to play hockey with them using the clouds as their rink.

Famous Canadian country music star Jay Smith, also known as Smitty Kingston, wrote a tribute song for the Humboldt Broncos called **Stick Out By The Door (Humboldt Strong)** that instantly went viral with millions of people streaming it. When Jay heard about Sequoyah's story he graciously dedicated a personal message and version of the song to Sequoyah, his father Kenny, and the Coastside Cougars.

We are asking everybody to please go to this tribute Facebook page tonight and post a picture of your "Light On and Stick Out By The Door" (or really anything you want to share if you do not have a hockey stick) and a message for Sequoyah. You can also see the video of Jay Smith personally singing the song to Sequoyah and Kenny:

www.facebook.com/SequoyahKlingele

Instagram: @sticksoutforsequoyah

We know Sequoyah is up there in Heaven kicking some major butt with the Humboldt Broncos by his side!

Thank you for all your love and prayers.

STICK OUT BY THE DOOR

By Jay Smith

DEDICATED TO
SEQUOYAH HUNTER KLINGELE,
HIS FATHER KENNY,
AND ALL HIS COASTSIDE
COUGAR HOCKEY TEAMMATES
AND COACHES

We left our sticks out at the rink
And signed all our names
With a bench for you to sit on
Just in case you wanted one more game
There's no referees or scoreboards
The periods never end
Use the clouds as a hockey rink
While you play with all your friends

All the hotel hallway games we played
Or Slapshot on the bus
There wasn't anything in this world
That meant this much to us
We'll use your tears to flood the rink
And your prayers to keep us warm
This won't be our last game
Yeah, we're still Cougars strong

Hey There Dad
Well I made it to the show
You always told me that I would
So don't you worry anymore
I've got my teammates by my side
So you don't have to cry

Just promise me one last thing:
You'll leave the light on
Put my stick out by the door

Sequoyah's stick out by the door

A Dedication From Heaven Where I Am Playing
With The Canadian Hockey Team

CHAPTER 17

The Memories Of a love never forgotten

Thank you with God's love. The family is guided through an unseen world. Tribulation, seven years of hell on earth living with the antichrist. Thank God I will be raptured.

Somebody loves you. It is so good to know that somebody loves you and that somebody's there.

Sometimes alone on the dark side of nowhere. Wondering when it is all going to end? Feeling the pain of the love disregarded, knowing the shame of living in sin. Somebody cares for you.

Sometimes the wings of an angel are the words of a friend, patiently waiting. So when your day is long, and the night is yours alone. When you're sure you've had enough of this life. Well, hang on, don't let yourself go. You're not alone.

Everybody cries, and everybody hurts sometimes, and sometimes everything is wrong.

Lord, it's so good to share your feelings with somebody who knows how you feel and care.

You make it easy to live life again in my world of misfortune. Somebody loves you; somebody dies for you and cares for you. So take comfort, my friend.

28 Sequoyah, playing with The Cougars Roller Hockey Team. And # 82 Sequoyah, playing with The Black Stars Ice Hockey Team. He displayed these numbers on his uniforms with honor and pride, seriously playing the game with professionalism.

Anonymous

Those words are so beautiful, Herb!. I hope you are healing well in the time of your loss. May they have him and feel him with holiness and righteousness. I'm so sorry for you, and I can't imagine the sorrow you and your family are experiencing! My prayers are with him and your family.

Anonymous

I know you have been in contact with my husband over the past few days, but I haven't had a chance to tell you how deeply sorry I am for your loss. Sequoyah was a wonderful boy, talented, loving with many potentials, with a zest for life, and loved by many. The many messages on Facebook testify to this.

The shock of his passing has touched so many; the compassionate ache in the hearts of so many of your friends for your painful loss shows care and concern for you and your family. This tragedy has been a reminder of just how vulnerable we all are, how quickly life changes.

I know you are on an emotional roller coaster, struggling to make sense of Sequoyah's passing. All who know my son and your family feel your worry and pain for my son's grief. If the tables were turned and my son was so tragically lost, I wouldn't know how to comfort my husband.

You know my son, and he can be volatile. If this had happened to him, I have no idea where his emotions would lead him, saying that I know you'll understand when I say I get your worry and concern for your son. The only thing I can tell you is to pray, pray for guidance and a way to help you; as you said, no father should have to bury his son, and no father should witness the suffering you see in identifying the body.

The wish to help him must be overpowering. A friend once told me that you never get over a loss, but you have to learn to live with it. I pray that you and your family will find peace in all of this and that, in time, the pain will not be unbearable or consuming.

God Bless you all; know that we are praying for you.

God's love is incomprehensible and vast, Far beyond our imagination or understanding. Sequoyah gave his life so others could live, a bright shining guardian angel treasure, one of God's elect.

Revelation 21; 4. And God will wipe away every tear from their eyes, and there shall be no more death, sorrow, or crying. No pain for the former things has passed away. 1 Thessalonians 4; 13. We grieve with hope and faith. 1 Peter 4; 8. "Above all, love each other deeply because love covers many sins."

He would not make any commitments until this is finished; trying my best to work on it favorably. It takes a lot of studying and praying to God to present this properly. This was not easy for my grandson because he was such a sweetheart, very kindhearted with love, and never said anything negative about anyone. And then to have his mother and uncle, with about ten others, give him the drugs, a $50 bill he had, and kill him. He was very impressionable and easily persuaded, he was the youngest one of the 10 people there in this drug house.

Romans 8; 28. "And we know that God causes everything to work together for the good of those who love God and are called according to His purpose for them. Matthew 11; 28. "Come to Me, all of you weary and burdened, and I will give you rest.

Psalms 91; 11. For God shall give his angels charge over you, to keep you in all your ways. Notice that "Angels" is plural, not singular. This means we each have at least two guardian angels. Grandpa needs all the help he can get, Emmanuelle Rose and Sequoyah Hunter. Please, God, protect me in all my ways and let my guardian angel treasures guide me and show me the light.

They have fun with their grandpa. And they are in thoughts, and heart, and spirit. And that love no one can take. And this love brings tears to my eyes for the friends that came together for the celebration of life. The family prays that everyone heard something they needed to hear or met someone they needed to complete.

This is a lot of love guiding my way. All two of these grandchildren were too precious and too young, although God knew that we needed some love in our lives and did not realize it until it was gone. When you're around someone you care about and love, let them know how proud you are of them.

The love that Sequoyah brought together cannot be measured or understood. God's love is beyond our comprehension or imagination. The miracle, God's love, is overwhelmingly present. Nothing happens perchance. Everything happens for a God-given reason.

Sequoyah, it was time to go home, and God took him by the hand; so many others could be saved through Sequoyah's precious memories and love. God's love for an angel. God's love is revealed through this dimension of love for Sequoyah.

Miraculously with blessed passion, faith, and prayers, nothing more intriguing or mesmerizing entices the soul other than the anointed love that comes from God through the Holy Spirit and Jesus Christ our Lord.

Dedicate my life as a grieving grandfather to my only son Kenny and my grandson Sequoyah.

The family would like to give a special appreciation to loving-kindness, who graciously helped our family through a time that no one should have to go through. This is personal and reaching out to each family member through the grace of God.

We may never know as this family moves forward going through the stages of death. Denial. Anger. Bargaining. Depression. Acceptance. In a heart-wrenching time, they were losing an angel sent into our lives to show us, love.

Life vibrates with love, a guide through the unseen world where angels go freely. Any time we think of you, the one thing that we do is thank the Lord, and then we say a little prayer for you. We ask God to watch over you and shine your light before our way, even though we are apart, but most of all, we thank God for your kind and caring heart.

An Angel, unaware, touched those who Sequoyah loved. A divine creation through the grace of God. Brought God's love into this world for a short time. With loving-kindness, a beam of light that Sequoyah brought into lives.

We came together to laugh, love, work, and play. Accepted God's grace that brought us together this way. We found that piece at the close of each day. Our parting has not left a void for a reason, and we remember the joy.

A friendship shared, laughing; oh yes, these things we do miss. However, a time we have spent together through God's holy grace and all the things we have in common will bring us together again one day.

The entire family feels deeply thankful and blessed for the special, unique, amazing precious friends with loving-kindness that came into our lives to support this family. For the passing of a great young man Sequoyah Hunter.

Your prayers are amazing, and the support is uplifting and comforted and brought some joy to our souls as we would like to share a piece of ours in this miraculous moment. Our sincere thanks for the fantastic support. Our souls genuinely love your souls with reverence, kindness, and prayers.

CHAPTER 18

Football

Playing baseball and football was the catalyst to move forward to hockey, which I found my calling. I want to thank all my baseball and football friends that showed me how to be a team and play together. My cousin Nicholas and Sequoyah played football together at a very early age.

Cousin Nicholas (68) Sequoyah (28)
played for the coast side cougars pop warner football team together

Football Skirmish

Sequoyah
Trying on my football helmet for the first time
finding it a little uncomfortable

I'm getting better and becoming a natural

The Football Game
Don't Give Me No Dirty Looks
Just Get Out In The Kitchen And Cook

Don't Even Think About Taking Me Down

Come And Get It

Not Today

If This Is All, You Have To Offer
Pick Up The Paper And Take Out The Trash

Put On Your Coat Put On Your Hat
Bring In The Dog Throughout The Cat,
Get On Down To The Laundromat

Sequoyah/Right Guard/Number 28

CHAPTER 19

Hockey My Dream

Professional Ice Hockey Player? Sequoyah, Grandpa's grandson, was always a joy to be around and fun. Sequoyah always had a smile on his face, and he loved everyone around him.

Grandpa attended a few ice hockey games that Sequoyah played in, Sequoyah's God-given gift. Ice hockey is a sport that can be very aggressive. As soonest Sequoyah stepped on the ice, it was on. Sequoyah was a natural at 16 years old, 6 feet tall, and 200 pounds. And very well could have been a professional quickly. The other teams were frightened of him. Sequoyah's dad and grandpa attended ice hockey games together to watch Sequoyah.

My life's been full and savored a dream of this love of my friend, and the good times one day will never draw to an end.

Sequoyah Hunter is in the big league. When he was a kid, he'd be up at 5 AM. Take shots till eight and make the thing drive. Out after school and make on the ice. That was his life; he would play in the big league, the big league. Not many ways out of this cold small town. You work in the trees and get laid in the ground. And if you're going to jump, it will be with the game. Real fast and brutal is the only clear lane to the big league. You left me alone in that house when I needed you most as you ran like a ghost.

Soul Hunter is released to go freely. God has placed an assignment and the calling for an angel. His name "Is Sequoyah Hunter." Like he played ice hockey seriously with professionalism. Sequoyah is hunting souls.

Sequoyah Hunter Klingele
#82 Showing A Stance Of A Professional Ice Hockey Player
Charcoal/Intimidation

Sequoyah
California State Champions/Ice Hockey/The Black Stars Ice Hockey Team
Deservingly So Exhibits The Metal Around His Neck

Sequoyah #28
2019 State Champions

Sequoyah
Has That Look On His Face That Other Teams And Players Fear

Sequoyah
With Pride Honoring The Fallen Veterans 2019, The Hockey Challenge

Sequoyah
Sends a hard check to an opposing team member
just to let the player know to stay down and do not get back up
this is not a game for the light-hearted
it's called a process of elimination; only the strong survive

The Cougars Roller Hockey Team Posing With
The British Roller Hockey Team

Sequoyah #28
Moon Bay Cougars Picture Taken 2017 The Junior Olympics

Sequoyah
Hard Practice Getting In Shape

Sequoyah #28 Center Back Row Tallest Player
Taking A Team Picture Before A Game As You Can See In The Background
The High School Is Ready And Backing Their Team Members

Sequoyah Holding A Shivering Little Dog
While Taking A Picture With A Friend And A Team Member
My Dad In The Background Having Some Boy Fun
Only Because Holding A Quivering Dog

Sequoyah
Throwing A Hard Message To An Opposing Team Member

Sequoyah
Scored The Crucial Goal That Won The State Championship
And Front Page Picture And Write Up In The Local Newspaper

Sequoyah Headline Page Of The Local Business Entrepreneurs
You Would Think Sequoyah Would Get A Kickback For Promoting Business

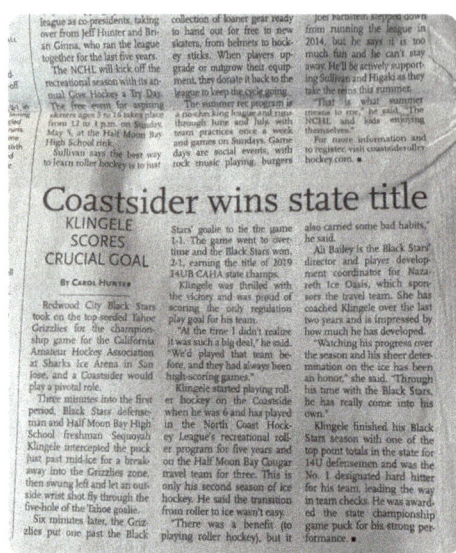

Sequoyah
Scored The Crucial Goal That Won The State Championship
This Write Up Following Front Page Picture Local Newspaper

Sequoyah Hunter Klingele #82
Playing Ice Hockey Team Called The Black Stars
For The 2018 Canadian/American Challenge Cup

Sequoyah Klingele #82
Black Stars State Champions 2019

Sequoyah #82
Passes The Hockey Puck To A Team Player

Sequoyah Klingele #82 Jockeys The Puck For Position
Notice Of Both Teams The Referees Made This Decision
Making Sequoyah Wear A White Helmet - Sequoyah Is Known Lethal
Sequoyah Was Severely Injuring Opposing Team Players Continuously

Sequoyah #82 Jockeys The Puck For Position
Notice Of Both Teams The Referees Made This Decision
That Sequoyah Wear A White Helmet - Sequoyah Is Known Lethal
Sequoyah Was Severely Injuring Opposing Team Players Continuously

Klingele #82
Showing A Stance Of A Professional Ice Hockey Player
Color/The Fans

My grandson – –Here's a clip of Sequoyah giving a hard check and getting a 12 minute major penalty. He is in a black Jersey #28 and the only player out there with a white helmet. This was last weekend in Tahoe. Tahoe is in first place we are in second place. It was first time we had played each other. The big showdow!!. We played them twice. Once on Saturday and a second game on Sunday. And this was about 4 minutes into the first period of the first game. Sequoyah sends a message with a hard check. Then a player from the other team hits Sequoyah in the leg with his stick, and Sequoyah turns around and gets in his face. Lol. Sequoyah had a tough weekend. Racked up more minutes in penalties in these two games than he did all season long in 26 games. Ended up getting ejected in the second game. The other team finally quit! The walked off the ice. Didnt finish the game. So **white helmet, black Jersey.** Enjoy!

Klingele #82 Playing the first place team in Lake Tahoe
Sequoia received more penalty time in these two games
then he did all season long in every game
the first place team walked off the ice

Klingele #82
Making it appear as though he was playing the game
I ended up tripping this opposing team player laying him flat out on the ice

Sequoyah Back into a white helmet, severely injuring the opposing player
sequoia is a player that you have to enjoy observing the sport of ice hockey

During An Ice Hockey Game, Klingele #82
Had broken one of the opposing team's player's leg, not just
breaking one leg but two, the rules of the game are when someone
gets seriously injured, everyone gets down on one knee

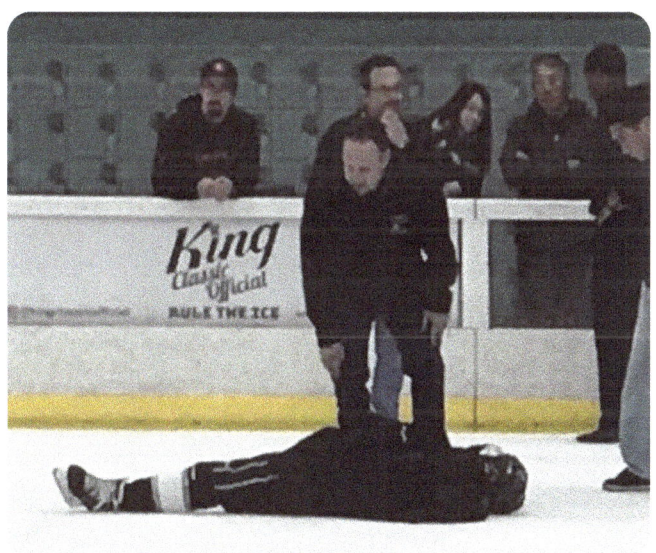

During An Ice Hockey Game, Klingele #82
They had broken one of the opposing team's player's legs,
waiting for medical attention. When the going gets tough, the
tough get going. This is not a game for the light-hearted

Medical attendance overseeing the injured player of the opposite team waiting to be transported to the hospital

An injured ice hockey player from the opposing team is being transported from the arena to the ambulance

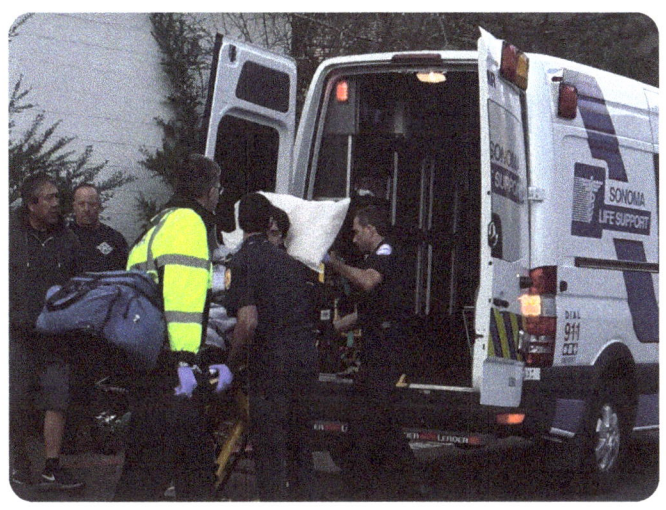

Opposing team member being loaded into the ambulance
headed for the hospital with a diagnosis of a broken leg

Klingele #82 White helmet, and this player is about to be injured
more time in the penalty box

Klingele #82 White Helmet Stipulates Danger
And Take A Chance. If You Care To Dance

White Helmet Notice Of The Opposing Players
Approaching Sequoyah With Caution

CHAPTER 20

The Enforcer

Playing the first-place team out of Lake Tahoe. Sequoyah takes the professional game of ice hockey seriously.

Natural spiritual gift, when the going gets tough, the tough get going soon as Sequoyah places his skates on the ice. It was my calling I found myself pursuing that game with enthusiasm. At 16 years old, 200 pounds, he was being scouted by professional ice hockey teams. Most certainly, I was playing college-level ice hockey.

The Lake Tahoe team was in the first place, winning 13 games straight. Because of my tenacity, they walked off the ice and never finished the game. I was the only one wearing the white helmet to let my team members know and the other teams of my reputation. Breaking the legs of two different opposing team players at two different ice hockey games is the game's name.

White Helmet To The Far Right Taking The Puck And
Starting Back Towards The Other Teams Net

All Alone Moving The Puck Along The Side
Opposite Team Members Waiting

A Player From The Opposite Team
Just So Happen To Get In My Way

Jockeying The Puck Back And Forth Heading
Right For The Opposite Team Player

The Extremely Fast Ice Hockey Game Very Difficult To Capture Pictures
In Sequence Knocking The Player Down That
I Was Right In My Line Of Fire

Then Getting Up And Skating Away, As You Will Notice The Referee
Blowing His Whistle With His Hand In The Air
Usually Means A Penalty And Time Spent In The Penalty Box

I Was Walking Away From The Incident When A Player From The Opposite
Team Came Up Behind Me
And Said Some Derogatory Remark Like I Was
Supposed To Be Scared Of Him

I Immediately Turn Around For His Lack Of Understanding Of
Whom I Was Getting Ready To Physically Get Into An Altercation

Not Hesitating For A Second, I Pushed Him Back And
Knowing If I Were To Get Physical
I Would Get Ejected From The Game And Possibly The Tournament

And That I Had A Few Words To Say To Him To See If
He Would Reciprocate Into A Physical Altercation, The
Referee Was Rushing Towards The Both Of Us

The Opposite Team Player Back Down,
And The Referee Was Getting Closer

The Referee Was Trying To Break The Both Of Us Up
I Was Not Ready Two Separate From This Opposite Team Player

It Appears As Though There Is A Problem With
Both Teams And The Referees

White Helmet Standing Above The Rest
Finally, The Referees Made A Decision To Spend
Some Time In The Penalty Box

Final Decision That I Go To Spend Some Time In The Penalty Box

Finally, I get in the penalty box, where I spent more times in this tournament in the penalty box than I have every game of the year, and finally, the opposite team walks off the ice. Their ego would not let them admit defeat. They have never played with a professional ice hockey player such as Sequoyah Hunter Klingele

CHAPTER 21

My Dad - My Family

I love my dad, and when my dad cries from his heart for missing me, it shows how much spiritual love my dad has for me, my three aunties, my grandma, and all my cousins. I love all of these precious souls the most, they show me the love I need the most, and I'm right here with you.

There's no reason to be lonely; know that I want you to be happy. And it's not your fault, and it's not grandpa's fault; the love that my life has brought into other's lives cannot be measured.

Realizing, of course, just as the twinkle of an eye and we will be together. There's no higher than to be in heaven with family members taken by God's hand.

Our parting has not left a void for a reason; we remember the joy and the fun. Dad, I wish you sunshine for tomorrow, showing you happiness and absolutely no sorrow. My life has been like a dream of this love that I will eternally have for my dad. Let our spirits bring joy, happiness, and peace with loving-kindness, and we will be together. But not yet. I love you.

Dad, we are shooting stars that have crossed each other's paths. With the glorious, miraculous light, we have touched a few souls. Showered Stardust on others will magnify God's love for generations to come. Briefly meaningful in the eyes of God, we are a divine creation of God, and we are children of God.

Dad, you are a beam of light that has entered my heart. And brought in the sunshine.

God has every star named and holds the oceans in his hand. And God's love has no beginning and has no end. It is eternal, going from horizon to horizon and touching our souls, bringing us together.

Dad, you deserve to be with someone who will make you happy. Somebody who does not complicate your life, and somebody who will not hurt you, and I will be right here by your side. God is preparing my dad for a life that he will understand why I had to leave him. I do not want my dad to be unhappy.

My dad's soul journey is something more significant, and my dad does not understand it yet. Unfortunately, I had to go through the pain of love and temporarily grieve my loss.

God's grace is freely given, and my dad will feel no pain, only joy and happiness, feeling a love that cannot be explained.

One day eternally, my dad and I will be in heaven with God, Jesus Christ our Lord, all the angels, saints, and prophets.

2 Corinthians 2; 4. For out of much affliction and anguish of heart, I wrote to you with many tears; not that you should be grieved, but that you might know the love I have more abundantly for you.

My Family

Beyond the comprehension or imagination, the supernatural's Miraculous Way, God, brings the right people into our lives at the right time. Friends who support, love, and pray for us, regardless of their circumstances. Anyone who does anything to help a child in their life, in our eyes, is a hero.

Sequoyah gave this family strength to preserve and warm our hearts. And Sequoyah would want all of those who came together to be nice to themselves because you're worth it, and the family love shown for Sequoyah is proud of all of our friends, family, and extended family.

We cannot put our prayers into words or express our thankfulness enough; God hears your heart. Ruth 1; 8. May the Lord reward you for your kindness. Keep the memories of all the good times we had together. I realize we were in each other's lives before God took me by the hand.

My Dad A Small Boy, With My Grandpa

My Dad, My Grandma, And Grandpa

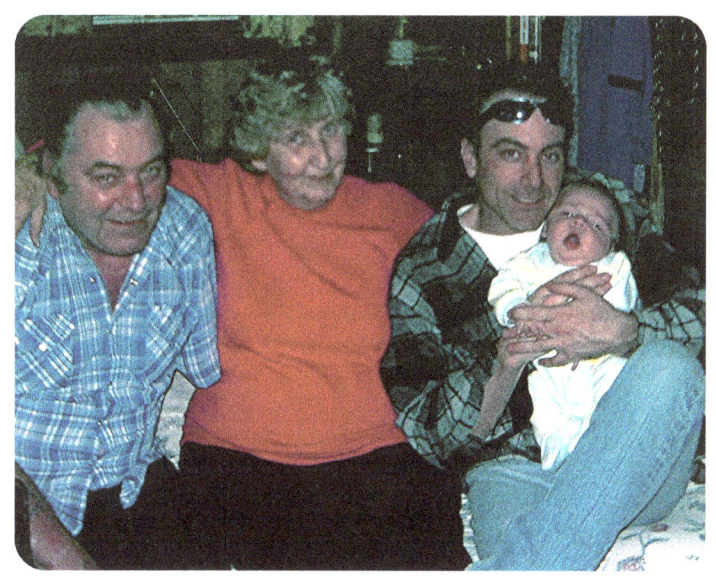

Fourth Generation Picture
Grandpa, My Great Grandma Ruth (my grandpa's mother),
and my dad holding me when I was newly born

My Dad And His Three Sisters My Aunties

My Grandpa's Bedroom, My Auntie Kelly, My Grandpa, Me Standing Up,
My Cousin Madeleine, My Cousin Sadie And My Cousin Coco

My Great Grandpa Park, Standing In A Hollow Redwood Tree,
My Cousin Sadie My Cousin Coco, And Myself

My Great Grandpa's Park, Standing In A Hollow Redwood Tree,
My Cousin Sadie My Cousin Coco, And Myself

Picture Taking In My Grandpa's Bedroom After My Service,
My Auntie Kelly, My Cousin Sadie, My Cousin Coco, And My Grandpa

My dad picked me up, and we love each other.

My dad taught me how to pose for a picture with a smile
the only question I have is, where are my shoes?

Enjoying a ride in my new fire truck

Two-year-old birthday party My Dad bought me
a brand-new 4 x 4, and I'm cruising

My Uncle Michael showed me how his nephew would look like in the future, playing professional ice hockey

My Dad And I are always happy when we are together

A friend of mine's puppy was so soft on a cold
winter day and was fun to play with

My cousin Michiah as you can tell, we were the best of friends
and the best cousins to each other we like each other

Grandma Taking Me Out On The Town

Uncle Russell attends a secret society meeting in the
mountains at an undisclosed location; no one ever knows
where my uncle Russell lives or is at; he shows up.

CHAPTER 22

My Service

10 April 2021 - Saturday 10 AM - Catholic Church - La Honda, CA 94020 - The celebration of Sequoyah's life. Sequoia Hunter Klingele - 12 October 2004 - 6 April 2021.

John 3; 16. God so loved the world that He gave His only begotten Son, that whosoever believes in Him should not perish but have everlasting life.

(For Kenny so loved Sequoyah that he gave his only son, that whosoever believes in Sequoyah shall not perish but have everlasting life). 2 Corinthians 5; 8. "We are confident, I say, and would prefer to be away from the body and at home with the Lord."

Looking at all the loving-kindness that came together for my service in remembrance with loving-kindness was almost surreal. I am so proud of every soul. So if you love someone or care about someone, make sure and let them know that you are proud of them. Let me repeat that, "I'm proud of you." It can instantly change a person's life by saying those words.

Although God had a love to show many others by sending angels and taking Sequoyah by the hand.

After the service, four gentlemen confronted the lady's son, who lived in his mother's house when my grandson was murdered. He pulled a rifle on them, and they called the Sheriff's Department. The sheriff's department came out, and the rifle was plain sight. He was on parole, so they arrested him. His bail was $250,000, and his mother had taken a $25,000 loan out on her home to get her son out of jail. And he is now hiding, and rightfully so.

When grandpa was leaving the service at the small-town Catholic Church, there was a stop sign at the bottom of the hill from the church, not two blocks away. And as God would have it, Sequoyah's uncle was, ducking low in his seat with his oversized cowboy hat on, in the passenger seat straight across the street at another stop sign, and his girlfriend was driving.

How can the uncle's girlfriend have an emergency when it appeared as though they were driving the church. And the only reason they decided to pretend like they were going to the church (after the service) is that grandpa had seen them.

Sequoyah's uncle's girlfriend called on the day of the service on the telephone to give her condolences, like the sleazy snake she is. After she knew my grandpa had seen both of them, and Grandpa asked the uncle's girlfriend why wasn't she at the service? She said she had an emergency.

My auntie Kathy was leaving the church with the funeral procession and stated that she never saw my uncle or his girlfriend. And eventually they drove straight past the church and hid.

The word of God is indisputable. Answer: Although he has persuaded many people that he doesn't exist, Satan is a real, personal being, the source of all unbelief and moral and spiritual evil. He is called by various names in the Bible, including Satan, meaning "adversary."

Sequoyah is a great spiritual gift to those who have ever had the opportunity to have known him. He always had a smile on his face and would reach out to anyone that needed a hand with loving-kindness. This young man gave his life so others could live. John 15; 13. Greater love has no man than this that a man lay down his life for his friends.

A Celebration Of Sequoyah's Life—Sequoyah Hunter Klingele
12 October 2004—6 April 2021

Sequoia Hunter – Shape Shift Trickster From The Ojibwe Nation
Soul Hunter For The Unjust Sequoyah Travels Stealth

Sequoyah's Two Nieces Had Just Seen Their Uncle,
And These Little Girls Just Know They Will Never See Their Uncle
Again That's All They Understand

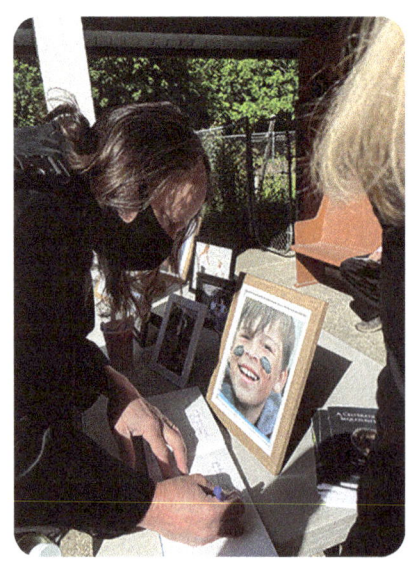

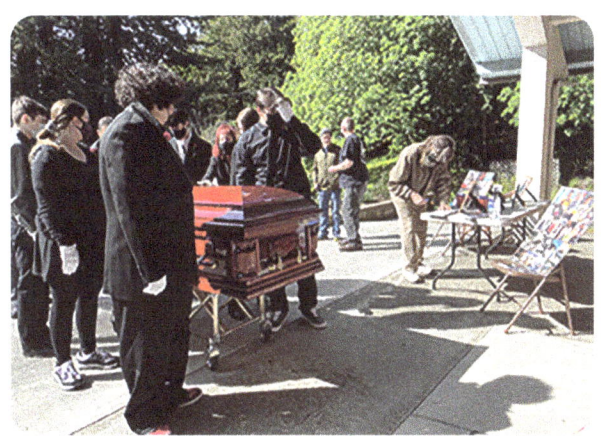

CHAPTER 23

My Sacred Holy Site

Sequoyah Hunter's Holy Site—Where Angels go Free.—The Family of Sequoyah, Graciously Appreciate the Guardian Angels who Shine Their Light and show the way with loving-kindness. I Sequoyah Hunter was born in Canada on the reservation of the Ojibwe Nation. 50% of my blood comes from Native American heritage. I am the Soul Hunter of the just and the unjust and a warrior for God/great spirit. The truth shall set you free. And there has no forgiveness of sins for the murderers of my soul. They have not confessed nor either forsaken their sins, never to do them again. I laid to rest on sacred holy ground with my great-grandpa, great-grandma, and two uncles.

> Mark 13; 32. But of that day and that hour knows no man, no, not the angels in heaven, neither the Son Jesus Christ our Lord, but God the Father only.

I Sequoyah Hunter. Blood and rights have given the honor to shape-shift and become a trickster for the unjust Hunting souls. Matthew 16; 27. For the Son of Man shall come in the glory of His Father with His angels, and then he shall reward every man according to his works.

> Proverbs 11; 7. When a wicked man dies, his expectations shall perish, and the hope of unjust men is parished.

The Route With The Hearst Transporting
My Body To The Holy Sacred Site

And Route With The Hearst Transporting My Body
To The Holy Site Along The Coast Highway

Laid To Rest Next To My Great Grandma

Laid To Rest Next To My Grandpa, My Uncle Tom, My Uncle Kevin

Overlooking My Holy Site It Is A Beautiful Day

The Setting Of God's Flowers Simply Breathtaking

My Dad With Immediate Family Grieving My Loss

My Sister Raven And Aunt Kimberly Native American Ceremonial

My Sister Raven

My Dad's Family And Friends Grieving Loss Of My Soul

Catholic Priest Ceremonial Prayers An Array Of Precious Flowers

Pallbearers Caring My Casket Over The Sacred Burial Site

Catholic Priests Ritual Procedure For My Holy Site

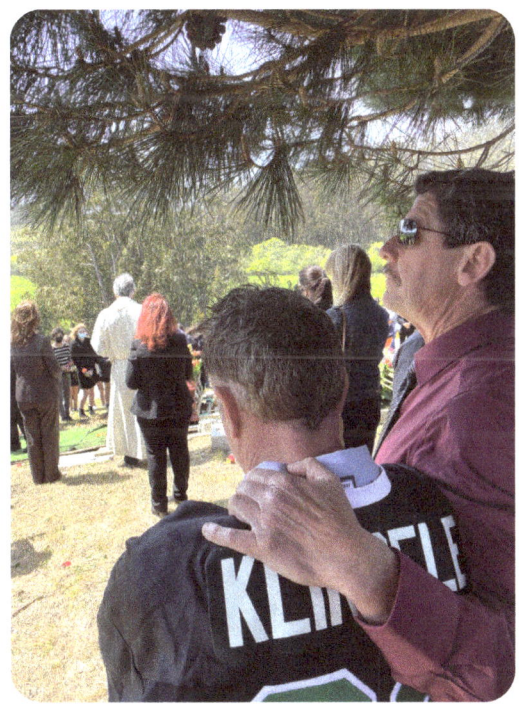

My Uncle Ross With His Arm Around My Dad

Catholic Priests Performs Prayers Over The Holy Burial Site Before My Body Is Lowered Into The Ground

Catholic Priest Places Holy Water On To The Casket Behind My Great-Grandmother

Catholic Priest Praying A Prophetic Blessing

My Auntie Kimberly And Uncle Daniel

Prayers Being Said By The Catholic Priest Where I Will
Be Laid To Rest Beside My Great-Grandmother

Pallbearers Place Their Clothes On Top Of My
Sacred Casket Grieving My Loss

My Dad And My Sister Raven, They Miss Me
With Precious Tears And Heartbreak

I Will See You Again One Day, My Friends But Not Just Yet

Family Friend, Where's My Hockey Shirt
With My Name And Numbers

Mother Teresa's Sisters Of Presentation

Laid Next To My Great Grandma

Laid To Rest In The Sweet Fragrance

My Dad And My Uncle Ross

My Auntie Kimberly

My Cousin Michiah

My Cousin Michiah And Her Dad Uncle Daniel Consoling Her

My Dad Being Hugged By Mother Teresa's Sister Of Presentation

My Dad Being Consoled Spiritually From
Mother Teresa's Sister Of Presentation

My Dad Hugging My Cousin Michiah

The Catholic Priest And Two Mother Teresa Sister Of Presentation

My Dad Holding The Precious Holy Cross Of Jesus Christ Our Lord
Who Shed His Blood For Our Wretched Sins

Mother Teresa Praying With Peace And Joy With Loving Kindness

2 Corinthians 5; 8-9.
For We Walk By Faith Not By Sight.
We Are Confident, I Say, And Willing Rather Be Absent
From The Body, And To Be Present With The Lord.

CHAPTER 24

My Dad's And My Home

Through the grace of God, my dad and I welcome family and friends that give their condolences with loving kindness and those precious souls who attended my service and grieved at my holy site. We have blessings and thanks for rest, with good food and loving friendship with gracious appreciation at the end of the day. All of my friends and family are God's reminder that there are angels who walk this earth.

My dad means a lot, and God answered my prayers by giving me a dad who is so kind and generous. My dad will be blessed with the most beautiful miracles in his life. Dad, I'm always right by your side. Think of all the good times we had together and the eternal life we will have. So please be happy to get some rest and patiently, please wait for the eternal blessing. 2 Corinthians 4; 18.—While we look not at the things which are seen, but at the things which are not seen; for the things which are seen are temporal, but the things which are not seen are eternal.

Sequoyah Hunter, blessed with "Agape," a love that cannot be explained, comprehended, or imagined, only comes through God's grace.

Some Things I Will Miss Shooting Hoop (basketball) With My Dad

As You Can Seem My Dad's Home In My Home Was Somewhat Secluded

My Dad At Our Home Grieving The Loss Of His
Only Son After The Holy Burial Site

Family And Friends Gathered
At My Dad's Home And My Home.

My Great Uncle Matt

CHAPTER 25

Preparation For My Dedication

To my friends, family, and the volunteers who so graciously volunteered their time, money, and resources to provide a dedication in remembrance of me, Sequoyah Hunter. There are no words of love that graciously express the feelings and blessings of love that have been shown so freely to me. All of these precious souls will be blessed miraculously through the grace of God, providing such an honorable attribute. At the high school that I attended, right next to the hockey rink. Possibly someday or any time, high school students need to remember that they are not alone. They can come here to this dedication and sit and reflect on the love and how blessed they are with God right by their side, and I will be sitting there as well, and they can come and talk to me. I was left in the flesh and taken by the hand of many angels that brought me into the presence of the Lord Jesus Christ. I was sent back here supernaturally in the spirit to care and be next to those who love me. And the teammates with who I played together signed their names and jersey numbers into the concrete leading up to the bench. I will always love you, and I will always be with you. Another is loving God's love; always keep in mind I will be here right by your side, and you will never be alone. God's gift to us is life; what we do with this life is our gift to God.

Loving Kindhearted Volunteers At The High School I
Attended Preparing A Bench In Memory Of Me

All Of My Cougar Hockey Friends Signed My Memorial
In Remembrance Of Me. Thank You, God

The Love Of The Volunteers Cannot Be Measured
Only Through The Grace Of God.

Loving Kindhearted Volunteers At The High School I
Attended Preparing A Bench In Memory Of Me

All Of My Cougar Hockey Friends Signed My Memorial
In Remembrance Of Me. Thank You, God

The Love Of The Volunteers Cannot Be Measured
Only Through The Grace Of God.

Loving Kindhearted Volunteers At The High School I
Attended Preparing A Bench In Memory Of Me

All Of My Cougar Hockey Friends Signed My Memorial
In Remembrance Of Me. Thank You, God

The Love Of The Volunteers Cannot Be Measured
Only Through The Grace Of God.

Loving Kindhearted Volunteers At The High School I
Attended Preparing A Bench In Memory Of Me

All Of My Cougar Hockey Friends Signed My Memorial
In Remembrance Of Me. Thank You, God

CHAPTER 26

Dedication from My Hockey Friends

The Coast-side Cougars Roller Hockey Team.

Invite you to honor our friend and teammate Sequoyah Hunter Klingele to unveil a memorial bench and hockey stick tribute.

High School Roller Hockey Rink. Half Moon Bay, CA.

Dear Sequoia,

We will leave our sticks out on the field and sign our names. We can play together one last game with the bench for you to sit on. There are no referees or scoreboards. The period never ends. Use the clouds in heaven as your rink. At the same time, you play forever with all your friends. Play in peace forever, number 28. Your coincide cougars roller hockey team.

Thank you to the following who donated time and resources to make this possible.

GoFundMe Fundraiser Team (Sequoyah's secret friend) Marina and her dad Stephen, Renée, Mayah, Sadie, Emma, and Ashley.

Smith Steelworks (Memorial Bench Design And Fabrication). Instant Display Cases, Half Moon Bay Building And Garden, Coach Mark And Family.

My Hockey Teammates And My Coach,
I Love All Of You, And We Will Be Together One Day But Not Yet

My Dad And My Auntie Kathy Sit Together On The Dedication Bench
At The High School Mourning My Loss Temporarily
Matthew 5; 5. Blessed Are The Meek; For They Shall Inherit The Earth

My Dad Reflects on My Loss
This Bench Was Dedicated To Know How Precious Life Is
Matthew 5; 6. Blessed Are They Which Do Hunger And
Thirst After Righteousness; For They Shall Be Filled

My Dad
Matthew 5; 7. Blessed Are The Merciful; For They Shall Obtain Mercy

My Dad
Matthew 5; 8. Blessed Are The Peer And Heart; For They Shall See God

My Teammates
Matthew 5; 9.—Blessed Are The Peacemakers; For
They Shall Be Called Children Of God

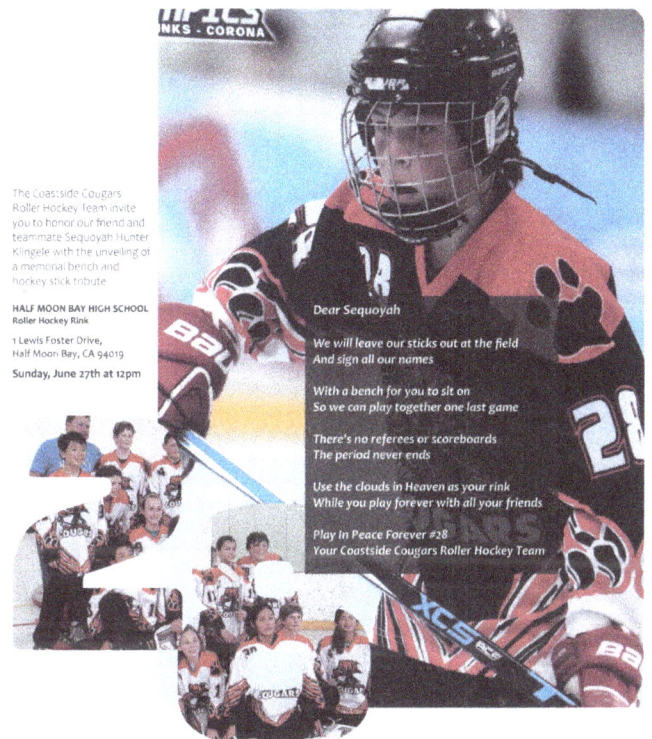

The Coastside Cougars Roller Hockey Team invite you to honor our friend and teammate Sequoyah Hunter Klingele with the unveiling of a memorial bench and hockey stick tribute.

HALF MOON BAY HIGH SCHOOL
Roller Hockey Rink

1 Lewis Foster Drive,
Half Moon Bay, CA 94019

Sunday, June 27th at 12pm

Dear Sequoyah

We will leave our sticks out at the field
And sign all our names

With a bench for you to sit on
So we can play together one last game

There's no referees or scoreboards
The period never ends

Use the clouds in Heaven as your rink
While you play forever with all your friends

Play In Peace Forever #28
Your Coastside Cougars Roller Hockey Team

A special thank you to the following who donated time and resources to make this possible:

GoFundMe Fundraiser Team (Sequoyah's Seacrest Friends) Marina Pokorny and her Dad Stephen Pokorny, Renee Casentini, Mayah Johnson, Sadie Nolan, Emma Steadman and Ashley Grant.

Smith Steelworks (memorial bench design and fabrication)
Instant Display Cases
Half Moon Bay Building and Garden
Coach Mark Modena and Family

My Teammate's Dedication To Me
Matthew 5; 10. Blessed Are They
Which Are Persecuted For Righteousness Sake;
For Theirs Is The Kingdom Of Heaven

CHAPTER 27

Worldwide Press

This April, a friend of Sequoyah's and a high school ice hockey player became concerned when Sequoyah Hunter wasn't responding to messages. The friend went looking for the 16-year-old and found him unresponsive in a house in California, a small town in the Santa Cruz Mountains.

The friend dialed 911, police records show. There was nothing emergency responders could do: Sequoyah Hunter, murdered?

Sequoyah's mother, struggling with drug addiction, left when he was young; his father said he raised their son.

Hockey was central to Sequoyah's life: Big for his age, he started playing in elementary school and excelled as a defenseman, winning the coveted game puck when his team won the state championships in 2019. In what would be his final season, his father drove him 90 minutes each way three times a week to practices and games.

Then the coronavirus pandemic hit, and his high school ice hockey spring tournaments were canceled.

Sequoyah struggled with the loss of structure. His dad, a tree service business owner, would leave for work early morning and return in the evening to find his son still in his room. His dad had bought him synthetic ice panels to practice on his own. Sequoyah showed little interest.

The father felt his son needed to socialize, so, in late 2020, he gave the teen more freedom—more, he says, than he would have otherwise. Sequoyah spent increasing amounts of time with his friends, staying overnight at his grandfather's in the family's RV park in the redwoods.

He said his dad had been preparing to get Sequoyah back to playing hockey once practice restarted. His dad noted that the sport would have consumed him as the level he played was highly competitive, and players would have been jockeying for college scholarships.

Instead, the father is now trying to piece together the last hours of his son's life. "No matter what happened, he would have said, 'Dad, it is my fault.' "But he's a kid. He still needed protecting."

My Dad Standing In My Room,
With My Life As My Dad Knew It And Grieving My Loss.

My Room Where I Lived With My Dad

A Few Of My Trophies Of Every Sport That Was Offered,
And I Played With Professionalism

My Dad Proudly Displays A Football Picture
In The Background With My Picture, Attribute Of My Love For Others

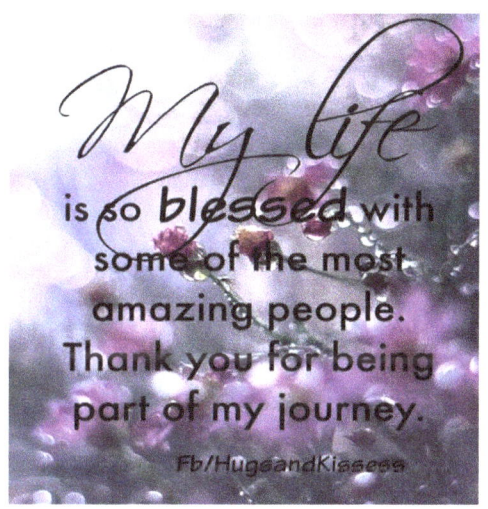

I Always Slept With My Favorite Stuffed Animal
Because It Reminded Me Of A Soft, Gentle Of
That This World Did Not Have To Offer

CHAPTER 28

A Celebration Of Sequoyah Hunter's Life

In remembrance of my grandson Sequoyah Hunter. 12 October 2004—6 April 2021. Church in the small town where Sequoyah resided with his grandpa. My grandson was a cool kid with a lot of love for others. He was a bright shining light and a precious Guardian Angel treasure. Those who cannot attend the service. The family appreciates your prayers.

Grandpa is proud of you, and let me regenerate the last words we said to one another, I love you, grandpa, and I love you, grandson. Have a good evening, and God bless.

On my birthday(4 April), attending church on Easter Sunday with my son Kenny and my grandson Sequoyah. And to have my grandson, who was staying with me at the time as he did, on the weekends because he worked bussing tables at a restaurant. On Easter Sunday, my grandson said to grandpa, hurry, grandpa, we will be late. Sorry, this makes me cry. Nothing happens perchance.

Sequoyah, born in Canada, was being scouted by a Professional Hockey Team. He was robbed of the opportunity and brought to his demise at 16 years of age.

Sequoyah's body was left in a drug house for hours. At the same time, close relatives and so-called friends cleaned up the drugs, paraphernalia, and cameras. Then making excuses and running.

I'm only 16 years old. When I needed all of you the most, you ran and left me alone in that house.

Mark 11; 25. And when you stand praying, forgive, if you have anything against any; that your father also in heaven may forgive you your trespasses. Luke 11; 4. And forgive us our sins, for we also forgive everyone indebted to us. And lead us not into temptation, but deliver us from evil. Psalms 25; 18. Look upon mine affliction and my pain, and forgive all my sins. Jeremiah 36; 3. It may be that the house of Judah will hear all the evil I propose to do unto them saith the Lord; that they may return every man from his evil way; that I may forgive their iniquity and their sin.

God needed an angel to show love, and there is the other side of God's love, God's wrath. Righteous indignation and spiritual discernment.

I am the family's guardian angel, hockey players, friends, and family members that are God's divine creation and children of God. And I am a soul hunter for God of the unjust children of the dark.

Revelation 3; 3.—"Remember, therefore, what you have received and heard; obey it, and repent. But if you do not wake up, I will come like a thief, and you. will not know at what time I will come to you."

Truth, Honesty, and Trust with loving-kindness. And God is all-knowing, watching all of His children, that they may do the next right thing. The last days of Sequoyah's life were the best days of his grandpa.

1 Kings 8; 50. And forgive the people that have sinned against you, and all their transgressions wherein they had transgressed against you, and give him compassion before them who carried them captive, that they may have compassion on them.

These emotional feelings will be going back and forth, never knowing when they will come up. The family would like to pray for everyone through the grace of God, the precious blood of Jesus Christ, and the Holy Spirit that moves throughout the earth that Jesus Christ our Lord left us with before ascending into heaven to answer all prayers. And between each of us helping one another.

Dealing with others who were not notified, which will extend on for a while, I had no idea what happened. And it's hard to know who those souls are until you get a telephone call, and they just start sobbing, in disbelief and denial, then the anger as to why they have not been notified.

So I'm having a tough time with my grandson's love for everyone, who never said anything negative about anybody. It must have broken his heart knowing he was going to die, and his mother and uncle and his best friends watched him die, and it must've been like Jesus Christ our Lord when he was being crucified after doing all those miracles, even his apostles denied him. Not on the physical torture. I feel the mentally broken heart was the pain. God bless.

Revelation 21; 1-3. "Then I saw a new heaven and a new earth, for the first heaven in the first earth had passed away, and the sea was no more. And

181

I heard a loud voice from the throne saying. "Behold, the dwelling place of God it is with man. God will dwell with them, and they will be his people, and God himself will be with them as their God".

And Jesus Christ forgave all of them. As a grandpa with my only son and my only grandson observing knows my grandson's mother and uncle killed him, I'm not so forgiving. God bless love with prayers.

Two things every soul can count on. We are going to die. And we are all going to stand in front of the judgment seat.

We feel our life is blessed with so many of the most amazing friends. Thank you for being a part of our journey. The more significant majority may not have the opportunity to meet such a great young man.

Sequoyah never said anything negative about anyone. Although playing ice hockey, he was most certainly faith with work. And the love this precious Guardian Angel treasure has shown with love. The family was overwhelmed by the friends and support through a tough time.

Romans 12; 15. "Rejoice with those who rejoice; mourn with those who mourn." Philippians 1; 30. We are in this struggle together. Philippians 4; 13. I can do all things through Christ who strengthens me." Philippians 3; 20—21. But we are citizens of heaven, where the Lord Jesus Christ lives.

It was amazing and so miraculous how God brings the right people into our lives at the right time. Friends who support, love, and pray for us, regardless of their circumstances.

It seems that Sequoyah is being taken home supernaturally through the grace of God miraculously. 6 April 2021,

Be nice yourself because you're worth it, and we are proud of you. No worry, no stress that his moment of happiness you will not get back. No resentments, no regrets; we cannot turn the clock backward. All we can do is move forward, grow along spiritual lines, and do the next right thing. God blessed with love and prayers the family.

Anyone who does anything to help a child in their life, in our eyes, is a hero. Sequoyah gave this family strength to preserve and warm our hearts. And Sequoyah would want all of the love shown for Sequoyah. We are proud of our friends, family, and extended family.

Everything is okay. The last moment is gone. The next moment is not here yet. Staying in the moment, everything is okay and reflecting on all the good memories. We cannot put our prayers into words or express our thankfulness enough; God hears your heart.

The greatest weakness of most humans is their hesitancy about how much they love them to tell others while they are alive.

If we do good things, good things will happen. If we do bad things, bad things will happen. Do more for others than you do for yourself. When is the last time you ask anyone, "is there anything I can do for you, or anything you need?" Keep God first, say your prayers, devote your lives to God, and service to help others. It is the year 2021, the year of our Lord Jesus Christ. Not disputed. Psalms 62; 1. My soul finds rest in God alone; my salvation comes from God.

Have a blessed, peaceful day with loving kindness. And I love you. Try not to let people, places, or things rent space in your head. You'll only give them the keys to your mind to keep you prisoner there. There is only room for you and God to light your way with Guardian Angels.

Now I lay me down to sleep, I pray the Lord my soul to keep, and if I should die before I awake, I pray the Lord my soul to take amen. Isaiah 33; 6. "He will be the sure foundation for your times, a rich store of salvation and wisdom and knowledge; the fear of the Lord is the key to this treasure."

And we are eagerly waiting for Him to return as our Savior. The Lord will take our weak mortal bodies and change them into glorious bodies like His own, using the same power, and He will bring everything under His control.

1 Peter 5; 7. God cares, cast all your care upon Him, for He cares for you. Job 5; 11. He sets on high those who are lowly, and those who mourn are lifted to safety. Hebrews Chapter 1. Jesus is God's messenger. As the radiance of God's glory. It is the exact representation of God. God sayings all things through His word. Provides the purification of sins. He is seated at the right hand of God. Is Superior to the Angels. Is God's son. Is the firstborn of all creation. Is God. Is king. Laid the foundation of the earth. Made the heavens; and is eternal. His throne will last forever.

Psalms 34; 18. "The Lord is near to the brokenhearted. The cards, the condolences of sorrow, the telephone calls, and some are still reaching out with no idea of this miraculous gracious love that Sequoyah Hunter has brought worldwide.

Psalms 31; 9. "Be gracious to Me, oh Lord, for I am distressed; my eye is wasted from grief; my soul and body also. Psalms 31; 7. "I will be glad and rejoice in Your love, for You saw my affliction, and You knew the anguish of my soul. Revelation 1; 18. "I am He who lives, and was dead, and behold I am alive forever. "John 14; 27. "Thankful for God's peace, spending each day living for everything and expecting nothing. Romans 6; 23. "For the wages of sin is death, but the gift of God is eternal life in Jesus Christ our Lord."

Romans 8; 18. The pain you've been feeling cannot compare to the joy coming.

"One day, Sequoyah asked his dad. "Why is it always the best people who die?" Sequoyah's dad answered, "son, if you are walking through a meadow of flowers, which flowers do you pick? The worst ones or the beautiful flowers?"

Sequoyah Hunter is an amazing beautiful soul who always goes all the way. He keeps his word, and he will give it his all. He will put himself last for those that he cares about. And rarely received the same compassion and effort in return. Yet, he continued to give freely. He was a giver and forgiver, very selfless with his love. And yet, he kept pushing forward, not letting this cold world change who he was.

Isn't it amazing how God brings the right people into your life at the right time. People who support, love and pray for you, regardless of your circumstances.

-Author Unknown-

AgapΩ

"ANYONE WHO
DOES
ANYTHING
TO HELP A
CHILD IN HIS
LIFE IS A HERO
TO ME."

– Fred Rogers
ITSALLYOUBOO.COM

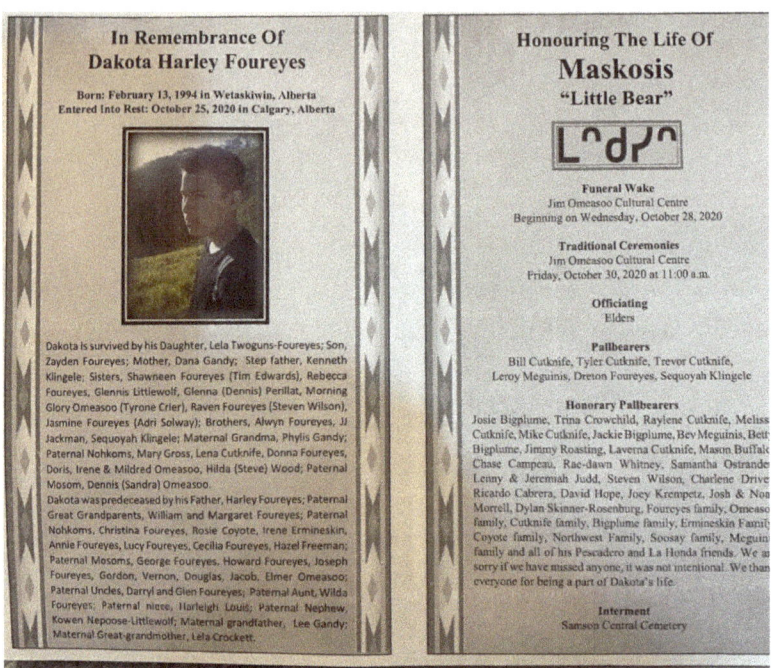

Sequoyah Hunter Klingele's Brother, Dakota Harley Foureyes,
13 February 1994/Passed On 25 October 2020 The Year Of Our Lord.
I, Sequoyah Hunter, Attended My Brothers Service
With My Dad And Sisters
I Am With My Brother, And We Are Guardian
Angels Of The Family Who Loves Us

Can You See Me Now

John 15; 13. There is no greater love than this, that one should give his life for his friend.

Sequoyah Hunter Klingele - Forever 16
10/12/04 – 04/06/21

We remember...

Matthew 13; 41. – The Son of Man shall send forth his angels, and they shall gather out of his kingdom all things that offend, and them which do iniquity.

2 Corinthians 2; 4. – For out of much affliction and anguish of heart, I wrote to you with many tears; not that you should be grieved, but that you might know the love I have more abundantly for you.

Can You See Me Now?
Sequoyah Hunter Klingele, 12 October 2004—6 April 2021

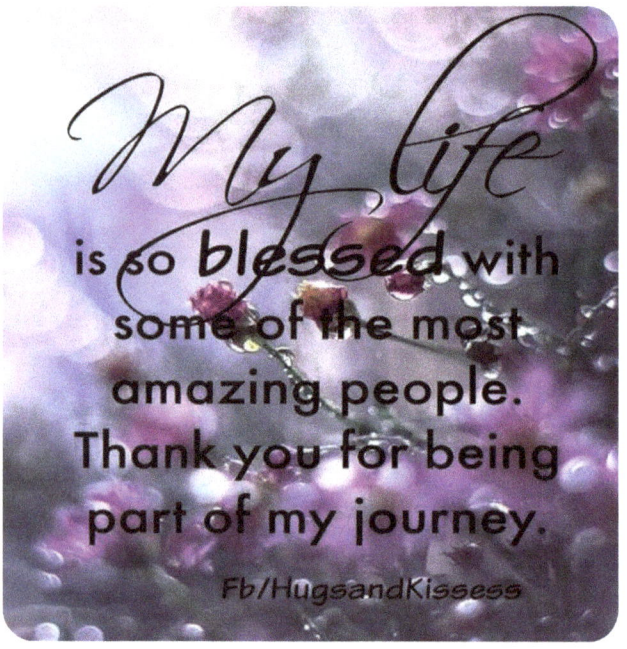

My life is so blessed with some of the most amazing people. Thank you for being part of my journey.

Fb/HugsandKissess

"My Headstone"

www.ingramcontent.com/pod-product-compliance
Lightning Source LLC
Chambersburg PA
CBHW051619120626
46551CB00014B/1864